Language for Economics

Integrated study skills and advanced
language practice

R. R. Jordan and F. I. Nixson

Collins ELT
London and Glasgow

Collins ELT
8 Grafton Street
London W1X 3LA

© R. R. Jordan and F. I. Nixson 1986

10 9 8 7 6 5 4

First published 1986
Reprinted 1987, 1988, 1989

Printed in Great Britain by
Bell and Bain Ltd., Glasgow

Designed by Jacky Wedgwood

ISBN 0 00 370330 4

Acknowledgements

Our grateful thanks go to students of economic
development at Manchester University who have, over
the years, provided feedback on material and have
contributed to its development.

We wish to acknowledge kind assistance with Appendix
3 from Jillian Taylor, formerly of, and Ranjan Ray,
currently in, the Department of Econometrics at
Manchester University.

We are grateful to Marilyn Oates and Jean Ashton for
their considerable help in the preparation of the
typescript for this book.

For Manchester economists the world over

Other books by R. R. Jordan

A Handbook for English Language Assistants
(with R. Mackay, Collins 1976)

Listening Comprehension and Note-Taking Course
(with K. James and A. J. Matthews, Collins 1979)

Reading in a Second Language
(with R. Mackay and B. Barkman, Newbury House 1979)

Looking for Information (Longman 1980)

Academic Writing Course (Collins 1980)

Figures in Language: Describe and Draw (Collins 1982)

Case Studies in ELT (editor, Collins 1983)

Active Listening (Collins 1984)

Developing Reference Skills (with Teresa O'Brien, Collins 1985)

Others books by F. I. Nixson

Economics of Change in Less Developed Countries
(with D. Colman, Philip Allan: Oxford 1978)

The Industrialisation of Less Developed Countries
(with C. H. Kirkpatrick – editors – Manchester University Press 1983)

Industrial Structure and Policy in Less Developed Countries
(with C. H. Kirkpatrick and N. Lee, Allen & Unwin 1984)

Contents

Contents of language exercises

Unit	Stage	Word study	Language use	Extension activities
1	1	*Exercise 1* Alternative vocabulary and explanation *Exercise 2* Economics *Exercise 3* Development *Exercise 4* Rise/raise/increase	*Exercise 1* Comparisons *Exercise 2* Definitions	
	2	*Exercise 1* Alternative vocabulary	*Exercise 1* Relative clauses *Exercise 2* Reduced relatives *Exercise 3* Summary	1 Writing: essay 2 Group activity: pyramid discussion: 'Economic development'
2	1	*Exercise 1* Alternative vocabulary *Exercise 2* Critic/criticise *Exercise 3* Synonyms and antonyms *Exercise 4* Pairs of words in economics	*Exercise 1* Verb tense: passive *Exercise 2* Passive: more practice	
	2	*Exercise 1* Alternative vocabulary *Exercise 2* Negative prefixes (1) *Exercise 3* Negative prefixes (2) *Exercise 4* Formation of adjectives	*Exercise 1* Reference skills: 1 *Exercise 2* Reference skills: 2 *Exercise 3* Summary	1 Writing: essay 2 Group activity: pairwork: questions
3	1	*Exercise 1* Alternative vocabulary *Exercise 2* Past tense forms	*Exercise 1* Prepositions *Exercise 2* The structure of narration	
	2	*Exercise 1* Alternative vocabulary	*Exercise 1* Verb tense: present simple *Exercise 2* Negatives *Exercise 3* Summary	1 Writing: essay 2 Group activity: pairwork and group work – discussion
4	1	*Exercise 1* Alternative vocabulary *Exercise 2* Continents, regions, countries and currencies	*Exercise 1* Plurality; fractions	
	2	*Exercise 1* Alternative vocabulary	*Exercise 1* Other, others, another	1 Writing: a case study 2 Group activity: pyramid discussion: 'Main causes of poverty in LDCs'
5	1	*Exercise 1* Alternative vocabulary	*Exercise 1* Prepositions with dates and figures *Exercise 2* Information transfer: a graph	

Unit	Stage	Word study	Language use	Extension activities
5	2	*Exercise 1* Alternative vocabulary *Exercise 2* Employ/ employment	*Exercise 1* Although and but *Exercise 2* Information transfer: a pie chart/diagram	1 Writing: essay 2 Group activity: discussion: role-play: 'Minimum wages'
6	1	*Exercise 1* Alternative vocabulary *Exercise 2* Industry/ industrialise/manufacture	*Exercise 1* Information transfer: a histogram or bar chart	
	2	*Exercise 1* Alternative vocabulary	*Exercise 1* Cause and effect *Exercise 2* Should: prescription	1 Writing: essay 2 Group activity: discussion: role-play: 'Industrialisation of a developing country'
7	1	*Exercise 1* Alternative vocabulary	*Exercise 1* More definitions *Exercise 2* Exemplification *Exercise 3* Back reference	
	2	*Exercise 1* Alternative vocabulary	*Exercise 1* Sequence: summary	1 Writing: a case study 2 Group activity: discussion: role-play: 'A transnational corporation'
8	1	*Exercise 1* Alternative vocabulary	*Exercise 1* Question forms *Exercise 2* Questions – further practice	
	2	*Exercise 1* Alternative vocabulary	*Exercise 1* Describing a diagram	1 Writing: essay 2 Group activity: pyramid discussion: 'Appropriate products for the consumption requirements of LDCs'
9	1	*Exercise 1* Alternative vocabulary		
	2	*Exercise 1* Alternative vocabulary	*Exercise 1* Commenting on data (tables)	1 Writing: essay 2 Group activity: discussion: 'World trade in the year 2000'
10	1	*Exercise 1* Alternative vocabulary	*Exercise 1* Commenting on data (continued)	
	2	*Exercise 1* Alternative vocabulary	*Exercise 1* Verbalising equations *Exercise 2* Academic caution	1 Writing: essay 2 Group activity: discussion: 'Inflation'

Note: Comprehension exercises occur after each Stage 1 and Stage 2 text; in addition, pre-questions occur before each Stage 2 text.

Introduction

Background

Manchester University has a long tradition of mounting postgraduate programmes in economics, and of providing English courses – both for overseas students. The material in this book has been developed by an academic economist and a language teacher who have worked with overseas students for several years.

Purpose of the book

The purpose of the course is to give practice in the English that is commonly used in economics studies: this includes grammatical features, vocabulary, language functions, study skills and the use of data. The language of the texts has not been simplified in any way and its academic style is typical of the kind that students of economics must face. The book also gives opportunities for extended writing and for spoken interaction by students in pairs, groups or classes.

The book is primarily intended for students who have already studied a basic course of economics in their own language and who will be following an advanced course of economics in English. In other words, economics as a subject will be familiar to the students, though the English language for it will not be so familiar. It is assumed that the students' knowledge of general English is at least intermediate. The students may be speakers of English either as a foreign language or as a second language (which is used as the medium of education).

The units

The topic-based units are concerned with economic development issues. The texts in each unit provide a fairly comprehensive overview and general introduction to the subject. The topics will be of interest to students in developed, as well as developing, countries, and should provide intellectual stimulation as well as language practice. Each unit has specific linguistic aims : these are listed in the *Contents of language exercises*.

Each unit is divided into two stages. Stage 1 consists of a shorter, introductory text on the unit topic. Stage 2 consists of a longer and more detailed text on the same topic, but this does *not* repeat the content of Stage 1; it also includes references for follow-up reading if required.

Overall structure of each unit

STAGE 1: Text (up to about 350 words)
Comprehension questions: true/false and open
Word study: alternative vocabulary and explanation; other exercises
Language use exercises

STAGE 2: Comprehension: pre-questions
Text (up to about 1,000 words)
Comprehension: post-questions
Word study: alternative vocabulary and explanation; other exercises
Language use exercises
Extension activities: writing – essay; group activity – discussion or role-play

Answer key and notes: at the back of the book

Notes for teachers : explanation of the exercises

Comprehension

For Stage 1 first read the text and then do the exercises. For Stage 2 first read the pre-questions: these will help to focus the reading. Some discussion at this point will show how far students can predict the answers. No writing is required for these questions. Then read the text, after which do the post-questions and other exercises.

Word study

Alternative vocabulary exercises help the student to understand the text, give practice in recognising synonyms, and help to increase the student's range of vocabulary (and are also useful if there is no good dictionary to hand). After the first three units, the format of these exercises changes. **Explanation** exercises check the student's ability to explain fairly standard economics expressions. Other word study exercises explain and practise vocabulary commonly used in economics, e.g. rise/raise/increase.

Language use

These exercises give practice in selected grammatical items, language functions, study skills and use of data. Sometimes, the exercises are labelled 'open': this means several answers are possible, and no answers appear in the key.

The exercises are listed alphabetically in the *Index to language use exercises* at the back of the book. If students have difficulty with certain grammatical features (e.g. present simple verb tense – Unit 3.2; past tense forms – Unit 3.1), they can do the exercises relating to these when necessary, out of sequence.

In the first three units only, specific practice is given in writing summaries. However, it would be useful practice for students to get into the habit of making notes from all the Stage 2 texts and then to write their own summaries based upon their notes. Examples of note-taking are shown in *Appendix 1 : Study skills*. The students should look carefully at this appendix before they do any extended writing.

Extension activities

These activities give opportunities to students to practise language in a less controlled way. This is done, firstly, through writing an academic essay related to the subject of the unit and, secondly, through various types of discussion techniques which are also related in some way to the theme of the unit. One particular discussion technique is the 'pyramid discussion'. There are three of these in the book (Units 1.2, 4.2, 8.2); the procedure is the same in each case and is described below.

Pyramid discussion A pyramid discussion is a device whereby students are encouraged to take part in discussion by gradually increasing the size of the discussion group, starting with the individual, then building up to two students, then four, then eight, until the whole group is involved. The procedure is as follows:

1 First, students should individually select three items, as instructed, from the list given in the exercise. The order of their three choices is not important.

2 Then each student, in turn, should call out the numbers of his/her choices. Write these on the blackboard for all to see.

e.g.	*student*	A	B	C	D	etc.
	choices	12	3	4	1	
		14	7	7	7	
		20	10	12	10	

3 After this, put the students in pairs so that they have, as far as possible, at least one choice in common (e.g. A and C, B and D above).

4 In pairs the students should then try to persuade each other to make changes in their choices so that at the end of a certain time limit (perhaps five minutes) they both agree on three choices. If necessary, they can compromise on new choices or 'trade-off' choices. The pairs' three choices are then noted on the blackboard.

5 Pairs should then be placed together who have at least one choice the same . . . and so the procedure continues until all of the class are involved.

6 If a pair or group finish their discussion before other groups, they can prepare arguments to defend their choices so that they are ready to meet another group.

7 While they are discussing, students will be practising the language of persuasion: agreement, disagreement, suggestion, qualification and compromise.

General

The first three units contain more exercises than the following units. This is deliberate : more language support is needed in the early stages. If you feel that there are too many exercises to do in class, some of them can be set for homework. For example, many of the **word study** and **language use** exercises are suitable for homework; so, also, are the essays in the **extension activities**. Class time can also be saved by requiring students to prepare the reading of the texts in advance.

Final note

Several appendices and glossaries, relevant to a study of economics, appear at the end of the book, together with an answer key and notes to the exercises.

The book can be used on an individual basis if desired, but for the discussion activities it is clearly necessary for several students at least to be involved. For some of the open exercises and the extension activities a teacher is obviously necessary (s/he need not be a specialist in economics).

Finally, if students need more practice generally with study skills in English, they are recommended to use the **Collins Study Skills in English** series of books and cassettes: *Listening Comprehension and Note-taking Course* (K. James, R. R. Jordan and A. J. Matthews), *Academic Writing Course* (R. R. Jordan), *Reading Comprehension Course* (D. D. Sim and B. Laufer-Dvorkin), *Speak to Learn* (K. James), *Developing Reference Skills* (Teresa O'Brien and R. R. Jordan), *Vocabulary Development* (D. D. Sim and B. Laufer-Dvorkin), *Answering Examination Questions* (P. Howe) and *Figures in Language* (R. R. Jordan).

R. R. Jordan and F. I. Nixson

Unit 1 The meaning of economic development

Stage 1 Economic growth

1 There is general agreement amongst economists concerned with the problems of less developed countries (LDCs) that a distinction should be made between economic growth and economic development.

Economic growth is defined as an increase in the productive capacity of
5 an economy over time, giving rise to an increase in real[1] National Income (NI). If the rate of growth of income is greater than the rate of growth of population, income *per capita* will also rise.

Economists distinguish between the Gross Domestic Product (GDP) and the Gross National Product (GNP) of an economy. GDP is the total final
10 output of goods and services produced within an economy for any given year, by both residents and non-residents. GNP is equal to GDP plus net factor (or property) incomes from abroad (that is, the difference between returns to the inhabitants of the country from property located overseas minus the returns accruing to foreigners from their property located within
15 the reporting country). For most LDCs, net property income from abroad is likely to be negative and thus GDP will be greater than GNP.

Both domestic product and national product can be expressed in net terms (that is, after allowing for capital depreciation) and either at market prices or factor costs (that is, including and excluding respectively, indirect
20 taxes net of subsidies). Net National Product (NNP) at factor cost is identical to ($\equiv$) National Income.

For many LDCs, economic growth has been rapid and sustained for much of the post-Second World War period. Table 1.1 shows that, in particular, the middle-income LDCs (60 countries with a *per capita* income of more than

TABLE 1.1   Economic growth

GNP per person (1980 dollars)[2]	1950	1960	1980
Industrial countries	4130	5580	10660
Middle-income countries	640	820	1580
Low-income countries	170	180	250

Average annual growth (per cent)	1950–1960		1960–1980
Industrial countries	3.1		3.3
Middle-income countries	2.5		3.3
Low-income countries	0.6		1.7

Source: World Bank (1981), Figure 1.1, p.6

25 $370 per annum) have made significant progress, although the low-income countries (36 with *per capita* incomes of less than $370 per annum) have been less successful. World Bank projections for the 1980s predict that higher rates of economic growth will be difficult to reach and sustain and that there will occur a widening in both the relative and absolute gaps

30 between the richest and the poorest countries, including the gap between the middle- and low-income LDCs.

---

[1] *Real income* is income that can be measured in terms of the real goods and services that it can buy. It can be calculated by dividing *money income* by a suitable index of prices.
[2] All figures are expressed in US dollars at 1980 prices, i.e. prices are constant.

Comprehension

A The following statements are based upon the information in the passage. If a statement is correct, write T (TRUE); if it is wrong, write F (FALSE).

1 Economic growth will cause an increase in real National Income.
2 National Income is the same as Net National Product at factor cost.
3 It is predicted for the 1980s that there will be no economic growth.
4 It is forecast for the 1980s that low-income LDCs will not grow as quickly as middle-income LDCs.

B Write brief answers to the following questions, obtaining your information from the passage.

1 What is the basic difference between real income and money income?
2 Under what circumstances will income *per capita* rise?
3 What is the difference between GNP and GDP?
4 Why is GDP likely to be greater than GNP in most LDCs?
5 What evidence in Table 1.1 shows that there was more economic growth in the period 1960–80 than in the period 1950–60?
6 Compare the growth of middle-income countries with both industrial and low-income countries in the period 1960–80. What conclusion do you reach?

Word study

Exercise 1A
Alternative vocabulary

The following words and phrases could be used in place of some of those in the text. They also explain the meaning of those words. For each word/phrase below write down the word/phrase that it could replace in the text. Also write the line number. Use a dictionary if necessary. Here is an example.
e.g. a difference – a distinction (line 2)

1 permanent residents
2 accumulation or coming as an addition of interest or profit
3 a fall or decrease in value
4 a prediction or plan of future possibilities
5 to forecast or prophesy
6 to maintain or continue
7 an increase
8 a difference or disparity

Exercise 1B
Explanation

The following phrases are taken from the text (line numbers are given). Can you explain their meaning as used in the text? Use a dictionary if necessary.

1 any given year (10)
2 indirect taxes (19)

Exercise 2
Economics

A   Notice in the text how the following words are used:
    economy, economist, economic

Other words related to these are also in common use:
    economics, to economise, economical

Note: Although *economic* and *economical* are both **adjectives** (i.e. they describe), *economic* is concerned with the subject 'economics' (e.g. trade, industry etc.), while *economical* means careful, or not wasteful, in the use of money or goods.

Use the six words (*economy, economist, economic, economics, economise, economical*) to complete the sentences below. Use each word once only.

1 It can be said that an early definition of _____ was 'An Inquiry into the Nature and Causes of the Wealth of Nations'.
2 The national _____ is the system of the management and use of resources of a country.
3 It is often possible to _____ if one compares the prices of items before buying them.
4 J. M. Keynes was a famous _____ .
5 Inflation may cause a country to be in a bad _____ state.
6 It is usually more _____ to buy large quantities of a product than small quantities.

B   It is not difficult to pronounce the six words correctly, but mistakes are often made by putting the main stress, or emphasis, on the wrong syllable in a word. Look carefully at the two lists below: the syllable that carries the main stress is underlined.

a 2nd syllable	**b 3rd syllable**
1 e<u>co</u>nomy	eco<u>no</u>mics
2 e<u>co</u>nomist	eco<u>no</u>mic
3 e<u>co</u>nomise	eco<u>no</u>mical

Practise saying these words until you can produce them all correctly.

Note: the first sound in 'economics' (and in <u>e</u>conomic, <u>e</u>conomical) can be pronounced as /iː/ (as in 's<u>ee</u>') or as /e/ (as in 't<u>en</u>').

Notice how the main stress changes in the following words:
    <u>in</u>dustry   in<u>dus</u>trial
    <u>po</u>litics   po<u>li</u>tical

Exercise 3
Development

Notice how the following words are used in the text:
  development   developed

Note that *LDC* = less developed country; *LDCs* = less developed countries. These words, and others that are related to them, come from the verb *to develop*. Several words which come from *develop* are shown on an approximate scale below.

to

▲ *development*
developed
developing
less developed } (countries) } These three are used interchangeably.
underdeveloped   *Developing* is more positive.
undeveloped

from │ *underdevelopment*

(Note that the first and last words are nouns, and the others are adjectives.)

Use the following words to complete the sentences below. Use each word once only.
  to develop, development, developed, less developed

1 The _____ countries are mainly agricultural primary producers whose economy is based on relatively primitive subsistence farming methods.
2 Such countries rely heavily on the export earnings from the sale of their primary products to the _____ countries.
3 It is usually advantageous for countries _____ their own manufacturing industries.
4 Many countries aim at _____, but few are successful.

Note: Various expressions are used to indicate categories of countries according to wealth or development:
e.g. developed   less developed
      industrialised non-industrialised
      'North'   'South'[1]
                      the Third World[2]
                      least developed (= very poor LDCs)

Exercise 4
Rise/raise/increase

In the text *an increase* (noun) and *to rise* (verb) are used. The use of these, and other closely related words, often causes difficulty.
Read carefully the following notes and examples.

A   Rise
1 *To rise* (verb intransitive i.e. used *without* a direct object)
  e.g. Prices continue *to rise*.
     The price of sugar *has risen* by a penny a kilo.
     The cost of living index *rose* by 10 per cent last year.

2 *A rise* (noun)
  e.g. There was *a rise* in prices caused by *a rise* in wages.
  Note: In the USA *a raise* is used instead of *a rise*.

---

[1]These terms were used in the Brandt Report published in 1980, *North–South: A Programme for Survival*. (The North, including Eastern Europe, has one quarter of the world's population but produces four fifths of its income. The South, including China, has three quarters of the world's population but produces only one fifth of its income.)
[2]This indicates the countries of Africa, Asia and Latin America collectively, especially when viewed as underdeveloped.

B   Raise

To raise (verb transitive i.e. takes a direct object)
e.g. The Finance Minister *raised* the tax on petrol in his last Budget.
   Bus fares *were raised* three times last year.
Note: In the USA the noun *a raise* exists, but this is rarely used in the UK.

C   Increase

1 *To increase* (verb transitive i.e. takes a direct object; and also
   intransitive).
      e.g. The Finance Minister *increased* the tax on petrol in his last Budget.
         It is estimated that the population *has increased* by 200,000 this
         year.

2 *An increase* (noun)
   e.g. There was a steady *increase* in population.
   Note: Increase (verb or noun) can often be used instead of *rise* or *raise*.
   For instance, it can be used in all the examples above.
   This can help to avoid some of the confusion between *rise* and *raise*.

Note:

1 In the text the verb *to give rise to* is used: this means to be the cause of,
   or to lead to.

2 The verb *to arise* is sometimes used: it means to come into existence, or
   to happen.
   e.g. A new difficulty *has arisen*.

3 The main parts of the verbs referred to above are as follows:

infinitive	*past tense*	*past participle*
to rise	rose	risen
to raise	raised	raised
to increase	increased	increased
to arise	arose	arisen

Now look at Table 1.1 in the text. The following sentences are based on the
information in it. Complete the sentences using the *correct forms* of the
following words: *rise, raise, increase*. Remember to decide if a verb or a
noun is required, which verb tense is appropriate, and whether to use
singular or plural.

1 Comparing 1960 with 1950, GNP per person in industrial countries
   _____ by $1450.
2 In 1960, compared with 1950, there was _____ of $180 in the GNP per
   person in middle-income countries.
3 From 1950 to 1960 the GNP per person was _____ by only $10 for the
   low-income countries.
4 In 1980 the GNP per person had continued _____ in all groups of
   countries.
5 From 1960 to 1980 there were sharp _____ in the GNP per person in
   industrial and middle-income countries compared with the _____ from
   1950 to 1960.

Language use

Exercise 1
Comparisons

A number of statements in the text make different kinds of comparison.
These are summarised on the next page together with others that are
frequently used. Read the examples carefully and note the language
constructions.

A   Some of the comparisons show *equivalence* (i.e. the same).
e.g. X is equal to Y. (=)
        X is identical to Y. (≡)
        X is the same as Y.
        X is the same price as Y.
        There are as many imports from X as from Y.
        There is as much money invested in A as in B.

B   Most comparisons show *non-equivalence* (i.e. not the same).
e.g. X is | greater | than Y. } (>)
          | higher |
        X is not | as | big as Y. } (<)
                 | so |
        There are not | as | many in X as in Y.
                      | so |
        There are | more | in A than in B.
                  | fewer |
        Policy A was | more | successful than policy B.
                     | less |

C   Many comparisons show one item or group compared with a number
(sometimes not fully expressed).
e.g. X is the | richest | country.
             | poorest |
        This is the | most | profitable investment.
                    | least |

Look at Table 1.1 and decide which words complete the following
sentences. Make sure that the words you use are in the appropriate
comparison form and correctly indicate the information given in the table.

1 In industrial countries the increase in GNP per person was _____
between 1950 and 1960 _____ between 1960 and 1980.
2 In low-income countries the increase in GNP per person was _____
between 1950 and 1960 _____ between 1960 and 1980.
3 In middle-income countries the increase in GNP per person was *not*
_____ between 1950 and 1960 _____ between 1960 and 1980.
4 The average annual growth between 1960 and 1980 was _____ in
industrial countries _____ in middle-income countries.
5 Of all the countries, the low-income countries showed _____ absolute[1]
increase in average annual growth between 1950 and 1980.
6 The industrial countries showed _____ absolute increase in average
annual growth between 1950 and 1980.

**Comparisons:
Open exercise**

In pairs or groups compose some questions based upon the information in
Table 1.1. Ask other students to answer the questions. Make sure that the
questions and/or the answers practise the different forms of comparison.
e.g. Which group of countries showed *the biggest* increase in GNP per
person between 1960 and 1980?

---

[1]An *absolute* increase is not the same as a *relative* increase. An *absolute increase* is a numerical
increase; a *relative increase* is an increase which has significance in relation to another figure
or measurement.

Exercise 2
Definitions

In the text some definitions are given. Two of them are reproduced below; look at them carefully.

1 *Economic growth* <u>is defined as</u> an increase in the productive capacity of an economy over time.

2 *GDP* <u>is</u> the total final output of goods and services produced within an economy for any given year.

1 Now write definitions for the following subjects using the information given. Write in the same style as definition (1) above.

   a *National income* – measure of the monetary value of the total flow of goods and services produced in an economy over a specified period of time.

   b *Elasticity* – measure of the degree of responsiveness of one variable to changes in another.

2 Look at the following definition. Notice the language construction:

Social economics *may be defined as the branch of* economics *which is concerned with* the measurement, causes and consequences of social problems.

Now write definitions for the following subjects using the notes given. Write in the same style as the example on 'social economics' above.

   a Statistics – mathematics – use of collected numbers which represent facts or measurements.

   b Econometrics – economics – the application of mathematical and statistical techniques to economic problems.

3 Open exercise Write some definitions of other economics terms that you are familiar with, in a similar way to any of the above.

Stage 2 Economic development

Comprehension

Pre-questions

Before you read the passage, read the following questions. Do you know the answers already? Discuss them briefly with other students to see if they know the answers. The questions will help to give a purpose to your reading; it is not necessary to write the answers.

1 Is economic development the same as economic growth?
2 Which criteria can be used to determine whether or not development is taking place?
3 What alternative ways are there for measuring economic development?

1   In the early years of the evolution of development economics as a distinct area of study, economic growth and economic development were generally seen as being synonymous. The deficiencies of using GNP *per capita* as an indicator of economic welfare (and by implication, the level of economic
5   development) were recognised by economists, however, and over time it became increasingly evident that economic growth on its own, although undoubtedly a *necessary* condition, was certainly not a *sufficient* condition to ensure increases in economic, let alone social, welfare.

Implicit within the concept of economic development was some notion of
10   progress. Economic development was thus taken to mean growth plus
structural and institutional change which involved the move towards certain
normative goals or objectives. Clearly, growth without development was a
possibility if increases in *per capita* incomes were not accompanied either by
structural changes or by the diffusion of the gains in real income among all
15   sectors of the population.

However, unless it is explicitly assumed that all sectors in the economy
grow at an equal rate so as to leave the proportions of the national economy
that they represent unchanged, the concept of economic growth as
consisting of continuous increases in total or *per capita* incomes *within*
20   *unchanged structures* cannot be defended. Economic growth will almost
inevitably lead to changes in the economic structure of the economy and
thus to define development as 'growth plus change' is not particularly
helpful.

With respect to the normative definition of development, it is in the work
25   of Dudley Seers (1972; 1979) that we find the most influential and widely
reproduced definition. For Seers,

'"Development" is inevitably a normative concept, almost a synonym for
improvement. To pretend otherwise is just to hide one's value judgements.'
(Seers, 1972, p. 22)

30   Posing the question, 'Where are these values to come from?', Seers
replies:

'Surely the values we need are staring us in the face, as soon as we ask
ourselves: what are the necessary conditions for a universally acceptable aim,
the realization of the potential of human personality?'
35   (Seers, 1972, p. 22)

The criteria that Seers suggests should be used to judge whether or not
development is taking place relate to poverty, inequality and unemployment. Other indicators relate to the political, social and educational
dimensions of development and in the Postscript to the re-published article
40   (Seers, 1979, pp. 27–8), a further dimension is added – 'development now
implies, *inter alia*, reducing cultural dependence on one or more of the great
powers.' Self-reliance thus becomes a crucial element in the contemporary
concept of development.

Seer's conception of economic development has been adapted and ex-
45   tended by a number of authors (see, for example, the Brandt Commission
Report, 1980, p. 23), and it remains the basis of what most development
specialists would argue that economic development *should* be about.

Difficulties arise, however, when the attempt is made to assess the extent
to which such objectives are in practice being realised. Hicks and Streeten
50   (1979, p. 568) identify and review four different approaches to the problem
of measurement, namely:

1 adjustments to GNP in order to capture some of the welfare aspects of
   development and improve international comparability;
2 social indicators which attempt to define non-monetary measures of
55   social progress;

3 social accounting systems which attempt to provide a framework for some of the social indicators; and,

4 the development of composite indices which attempt to combine various social indicators into a single index of human and social development (the
60 'quality of life').

They conclude:

> 'Attempts to introduce other costs and benefits of development, which would move GNP toward a broader welfare measure, lack a logical basis and tend instead to result in a confusion of concepts. Research on *'social' indicators* has
65 failed to produce an alternative which is as readily accepted and comprehended as GNP per head ... Systems of *social accounts* which could integrate social indicators through some unifying concept have not been able to overcome successfully all the difficult problems encountered.
>   ... The search for a composite index of social welfare, analogous to GNP
70 as an index of production, has been a fruitless one so far, since it has proved virtually impossible to translate every aspect of social progress into money values or some other readily accepted common denominator. The great deal of work devoted to composite indices, however, suggests the need for a single number which, like GNP per head, can be quickly grasped and gives a rough
75 indication of "social" development.'

(Hicks and Streeten, 1979, p. 577)

The recognition that economic growth does not automatically solve problems relating to poverty, inequality and unemployment has been an important step forward in the evolution of development studies. But the
80 normative, essentially utopian, definition of development itself creates problems. 'Seers-type' definitions of development refer to an ideal world or state of affairs and, as a consequence, are both ahistorical and apolitical – ahistorical because they postulate idealised structures that do not, and never have, existed, and apolitical because development is defined in an
85 abstract sense and is not related to any particular political/social/economic structure.

The division of the world into developed and less developed countries, and the utilisation of an idealised concept of development, imply that the developed countries have in some sense 'solved' the problems of develop-
90 ment, whereas clearly this is not the case. In addition, the popular, normative concept of development denies the specificity of the processes of growth and change that are occurring in contemporary LDCs. We will develop this point further in Unit 2.

References

Brandt Commission Report (1980), *North–South: A Programme for Survival*, London, Pan Books.

Hicks, N. & Streeten, P. (1979), 'Indicators of Development: The Search for a Basic Needs Yardstick', *World Development*, Vol. 7, No. 6, June.

Seers, D. (1972), 'What Are We Trying to Measure?', in Baster, N. (ed.) (1972), *Measuring Development*, London, Frank Cass; reprinted in Lehmann, D. (ed.) (1979), *Development Theory: Four Critical Studies*, London, Frank Cass.

World Bank (1981), *World Development Report 1981*, New York, Oxford University Press.

Comprehension

Post-questions

After you have read the passage write brief answers to the following questions. Try to express your answers in your own words if possible.

1 In what ways, in theory at least, might there be growth without development?
2 Under what circumstances might it be possible for economic growth to consist of continuous increases in total or *per capita* incomes within unchanged structures?
3 In addition to poverty, inequality and unemployment, what other indicators or elements of development feature in the work of Dudley Seers?
4 Why is none of the four approaches to measuring development satisfactory?
5 What seems to be the main problem with the 'Seers-type' definitions of development?

Word study

**Exercise 1A
Alternative vocabulary**

Below is a list of words (and line numbers) from the text (1–16). Next to them is a list of synonyms (words or phrases with the same meaning) or explanations, in mixed order (a–p). Match the words from the text with their synonyms.

1 distinct (1)	a fully and clearly stated
2 deficiencies (3)	b similar to
3 implicit (9)	c ideal or perfect
4 normative (12)	d separate
5 diffusion (14)	e not related to history
6 explicitly (16)	f implied or suggested
7 postscript (39)	g without a political dimension
8 crucial (42)	h propose something (which has not been proved) as a basis for reasoning
9 adapted (44)	i prescriptive, incorporating value judgments
10 composite (58)	j made up of several parts; compound
11 analogous (69)	k spreading or dispersion
12 fruitless (70)	l very important, or decisive.
13 utopian (80)	m unsuccessful, useless
14 ahistorical (82)	n defects, inadequacies
15 apolitical (82)	o modified, altered
16 postulate (83)	p additional section, supplement

**Exercise 1B
Explanation**

The following phrases are taken from the text (line numbers are given). Can you explain their meaning as used in the text? Use a dictionary if necessary.
1 value judgements (28)   3 common denominator (72)
2 criteria (36)

Language use

**Exercise 1
Relative clauses**

Notice how the two following sentences can be joined together:

Agriculture employs a large number of workers.
The workers are often poorly paid.

= Agriculture employs a large number of workers *who* are often poorly paid.

By joining the sentences in this way the noun *workers* is not repeated. The **relative pronoun** *who* is used, followed by the words which describe *workers* (which form a **relative clause**). The purpose of the relative clause is often to give extra or more detailed information, or to be more precise. In the texts in Stages 1 and 2 a number of relative clauses are used: *who* refers to persons; *which* refers to things; *that* also refers to things (and sometimes persons).

Join the following pairs of sentences together: make the second sentence in each pair a relative clause of the first sentence. Write out the new sentence, putting the relative clause in the correct place (next to the correct noun), and choosing the correct pronoun (*who* or *which*).

1 In many LDCs agriculture is very inefficient.
   Agriculture is the largest sector.

2 Economic growth is not a sufficient condition on its own to ensure an increase in economic welfare.
   Economic growth is a necessary condition for economic development.

3 Dudley Seers has influenced the thinking of many economists.
   He has defined development as almost a synonym for improvement.

4 Development can be determined by various criteria.
   The criteria relate to poverty, inequality, unemployment and self-reliance.

5 Hicks and Streeten conclude that there is no viable alternative to using GNP at present.
   Hicks and Streeten have analysed four different approaches to the problem of measuring development.

Exercise 2
Reduced relative clauses

It is sometimes possible for a **reduced relative clause** to be used instead of a full clause. In this case the relative pronoun is omitted together with part of the verb. Look at these examples of reduced relative clauses from the text in Stage 1:

A 'There is general agreement amongst *economists concerned with* the problems of LDCs . . .'

   '*who are*' has been omitted after 'economists' (i.e. 'economists who are concerned with . . .')

B 'GDP is the *total final output of goods and services produced* within an economy for any given year . . .'

   '*which is*' has been omitted after 'services' (*note:* 'which is' refers to 'total final output').

Can you find any examples of reduced relative clauses in the Stage 2 text? If so, write them down, noting the line number.

Exercise 3
Summary

The following passage is a summary of the Stage 2 text 'Economic development'. Complete the summary by writing down one word for each numbered space. The first one has been done as an example. Read the passage through quickly before writing anything. See if you can complete the summary without looking back. If you find this difficult, read the passage again.

There have been changes over time in the definitions of *economic* (1)_____ and (2)_____ (3)_____ .

In the early years, economic growth and economic development were seen as being synonymous. Then there were seen to be deficiencies in using (4)_____ (5)_____ (6)_____ as an indicator of, and economic growth on its own as a condition for, economic development. Later, economic development implied (7)_____ plus structural and institutional (8)_____ , moving towards certain (9)_____ goals or objectives.

Dudley Seers provides a widely held normative definition which takes as its (10)_____ poverty, inequality and unemployment. Other (11)_____ relate to the political, social and educational dimensions of development; (12)_____ has also become an important element.

There are problems, however, in measuring the degree of development. Hicks and Streeten refer to four approaches to this: (13)_____ to GNP, social indicators, social (14)_____ systems, and composite (15)_____ . None of the alternatives, however, has yet proved to be satisfactory.

Normative definitions of development create other problems. They refer to an (16)_____ world and, as a consequence, they do not relate to any particular country. In addition, the implication that developed countries have solved the problems of (17)_____ is clearly not true.

Extension activities

1 Writing : Essay

After you have finished reading Stages 1 and 2, and after the comprehension exercises, word study and language use sections have been completed, write a short essay on the following topic: 'What are the main problems associated with economic development?' See Appendix 1: Study skills (**A** Note-taking; **B** Writing an essay) for examples of note-taking based on the Stage 2 text and for information about writing this essay.

2 Group activity: Pyramid discussion

a Individually select the *three* most important requirements from the list below that you think will help a developing country to improve its economic development. The order of the three choices is not important. The time-scale of the items below in the process of economic development can be interpreted as you wish – either short- or long-term.

b The procedure for continuing this activity is described on page 8.

1 a good standard of education in schools for all (or most) children
2 adult literacy
3 a low birth rate
4 good health for the working population
5 a small percentage of the population employed in agriculture
6 modernisation of agricultural techniques
7 higher productivity per worker (in agriculture and industry)
8 a large amount of foreign aid
9 a high rate of import substitution
10 a high propensity to save
11 an effective tax system
12 greater equality of distribution of income
13 the growth of financial institutions
14 a high rate of investment in industry
15 government direction or control of investment and production
16 an increase in exports and export earnings
17 diversification of exports, especially exports of manufactured goods
18 an abundance of natural resources
19 more efficient allocation of scarce resources
20 political stability

Unit 2   An alternative approach: underdevelopment and development in a historical context

Stage 1   A critique of orthodox theory

1 Early theorising on economic development tended to be based, explicitly or implicitly, on a number of general principles, of which two need to be highlighted:

1 economic development meant progress towards certain well-defined
5   general objectives, usually corresponding to the specific conditions found in the advanced (capitalist) countries;
2 LDCs would progress towards that 'model' of development once they had overcome or eliminated certain economic, political, social and cultural obstacles retarding their advance.

10   (Dos Santos, 1973)

Rostow's *Stages of Economic Growth* (Rostow, 1962) is a classic illustration of the first point, and the concept of a 'vicious circle' retarding or preventing economic development illustrates the second.

The radical critics of orthodox development theory argued, however, that
15 it was wrong to see economic backwardness (or underdevelopment) merely as a stage *prior* to development, with all countries moving along one path in a similar direction, with some (the advanced countries) merely ahead of the others (the LDCs). Rather, it was argued, underdevelopment, far from constituting a backwardness prior to (capitalist) development, was in fact
20 *the product* of capitalist development in the metropolitan centres (Western Europe and North America). Development and underdevelopment were thus merely the opposite sides of the same coin (Frank, 1967).

Clearly, this alternative theoretical perspective requires that the emergence of economic backwardness and poverty be located and analysed within
25 a historical framework. The LDCs, with very few exceptions, have at one time or another been colonies of various metropolitan powers (the United Kingdom, France, Spain, Portugal, Belgium, etc.) and colonialism itself was seen not as a historical accident, but as the objective product of capitalism at a certain stage of its development (Szentes, 1971, Part 2,
30 Ch. 1).

The earliest period of colonialism was associated with piracy, plunder and slavery. As industrial capitalism emerged in Western Europe, an international division of labour was established within which the colonial possessions, now formally incorporated into the spheres of interest of the
35 metropolitan powers, became suppliers of raw materials and foodstuffs to those powers, provided captive markets for their manufactured goods and opportunities for profitable investment.

Comprehension

A   The following statements are based upon the information in the passage. If a statement is correct, write T (TRUE); if it is wrong, write F (FALSE).

1   Early theories of economic development were based on two general principles.
2   It was believed that after less developed countries (LDCs) had removed certain barriers slowing down their progress, they would advance towards development.
3   Rostow's *Stages of Economic Growth* illustrates well the second point made by Dos Santos.
4   The critics of conventional development theory said that it was wrong to view underdevelopment as a period just before development.
5   Critics have argued that underdevelopment in LDCs was the result of capitalist development in the industrialised countries.
6   Colonialism itself was not seen as the objective product of capitalism.
7   The European industrialised countries provided markets for the manufactured goods of the less developed countries.

B   Write brief answers to the following questions, obtaining your information from the passage.

1   Of what does Rostow's *Stages of Economic Growth* serve as a good example?
2   According to critics of orthodox development theory, underdevelopment did not merely form a stage prior to development. What did they say that underdevelopment really was?
3   What is the 'historical framework' for most of the LDCs?
4   What was the function of the colonies in the newly formed international division of labour?

Word study

Exercise 1A
Alternative vocabulary

The following words and phrases could be used in place of some of those in the text. They also explain the meaning of those words. For each word/phrase below write down the word/phrase in the text that it could replace. Also write the line number. Use a dictionary if necessary.

1   emphasised (or given prominence)   5   before
2   removed (or eradicated)   6   connected with
3   barriers   7   robbery at sea
4   slowing down (or hindering)   8   robbery with force (during a war)

Exercise 1B
Explanation

The following phrases are taken from the text (lines numbers are given). Can you explain their meaning? Use a dictionary if necessary.

1   a vicious circle (12)   4   spheres of interest (34)
2   opposite sides of the same coin (22)   5   captive markets (36)
3   division of labour (33)

Exercise 2
Critic/criticise

In the text there are two related words – a *critic*, and a *critique*.
A *critic* is a person who *criticises* something (from the verb *to criticise*).
A *critique* is an article (or academic writing) that *criticises* an idea or argument.
A *criticism* is a judgement of the qualities of something by a *critic*.

Note: Pronunciation: *critic* contains two 'short' i sounds (as in *it*). In *critique*, the second i is a 'long' sound (as in *tea*).

Use the following words to complete the sentences below. Use each word once only and change its form if necessary i.e. singular/plural etc.
   to criticise, criticism, critic, critique.

1 Many _____ of development theories have argued against using models based on capitalism.
2 Many of the _____ made of development theories would seem to be justified.
3 Karl Marx wrote several _____ of the ideas and theories of other economists and political philosophers.
4 It is easier _____ theories than to propound (propose) them.

Exercise 3
Pairs of words –
synonyms and antonyms

In the text there are several words that are commonly used when describing or commenting on theories or other similar abstract terms. These are set out below in table 1.

1

adjective	noun
orthodox	theory
radical	concept

orthodox   meaning – having opinions or beliefs which are generally accepted or approved.
radical   meaning – favouring fundamental reforms; advanced in opinions and policies.

In some ways *orthodox* and *radical* can be considered as 'opposites' (**antonyms**). Thus 'an orthodox theory or concept' could be the 'opposite' of 'a radical concept or theory'. Other words that are used in a similar way are shown in table 2.

2

adjective	noun
conventional	view
traditional	opinion
reactionary	belief
fundamental	idea
advanced	notion
progressive	policy
revolutionary	
established	

In some contexts *radical* and *advanced* can be considered to be very similar or the same (**synonyms**).

1 Use your dictionary to find out which adjectives are synonyms and which are antonyms.
2 Write sentences of your own using some of the words from the tables, e.g. Many radical ideas are difficult to accept at first.

Exercise 4
Pairs of words in economics

There are a number of words in economics that are best learned in pairs (you may think of them as 'opposites'): e.g. *supply* and *demand*, *maximum* and *minimum*. Sometimes the words are joined together (hyphenated): e.g. *large-scale* and *small-scale*, *capital-intensive* and *labour-intensive*, *long-term* and *short-term*; sometimes they are separate words: e.g. *long run* and *short run*. Sometimes particular words are used with certain economics terms: e.g. a *favourable*, or *adverse*, *balance of trade*.

In the following table some of the more commonly used pairs of words are shown in mixed order. Match each word on the right to its 'opposite' on the left. If you are not sure what the words mean, check them in a dictionary or a dictionary of economics (see the introduction to the glossary of economics terms).

1 absolute	14 input	a invisible	n debit
2 asset	15 internal	b sufficient	o cyclical
3 bilateral	16 lend	c revaluation	p appreciation
4 competitive	17 necessary	d rural	q dynamic
5 credit	18 production	e relative	r external
6 depreciation	19 retail	f wholesale	s exogenous
7 devaluation	20 revenue	g horizontal	t export
8 endogenous	21 secular	h liability	u consumption
9 equilibrium	22 static	i output	v deflation
10 gross	23 surplus	j multilateral	w heterogeneous
11 homogeneous	24 vertical	k expenditure	x borrow
12 import	25 visible	l deficit	y disequilibrium
13 inflation	26 urban	m complementary	z net

Language use

Exercise 1
Verb tense: passive

The text discusses economic theories that were proposed in the past. In such an academic discussion or description, the verb form that is used is frequently the **past simple passive** (e.g. . . . *were proposed* in the previous sentence). This verb form is more impersonal and, therefore, more suitable for academic writing. Compare the following:

active, past   We highlighted two principles . . . (focuses attention on *we*)
passive, past   Two principles *were highlighted* . . . (focuses attention on *principles* and *highlighted*)

The following sentences have been taken from the text and modified. Rewrite each sentence putting the verb (given in brackets at the end) in the correct form (i.e. singular or plural) in the past simple passive (remember . . . *was* or *were* + past participle).

1 There were specific conditions which _____ in the advanced countries. (find)

2 It _____ that underdevelopment was the product of capitalist development. (argue)

3 The emergence of economic backwardness _____ within a historical framework. (locate)

4 Colonialism _____ as the objective product of capitalism. (see)

5 The earliest period of colonialism _____ with piracy, plunder and slavery. (associate)

6 Captive markets _____ by the colonies for the metropolitan powers. (provide).

Exercise 2
Passive: more practice

The following passage is a summary of the Stage 1 text. Complete the passage by choosing one of the verbs from the following list for each numbered space. Put the verb in the correct passive form – *was* or *were* + past participle (e.g. *were proposed*).

    assume, base, cause, colonise, consider, establish, manufacture, overcome, supply

Early theories on economic development (1)_____ on several general principles. It (2)_____ that development involved imitating the advanced countries after a number of difficulties (3)_____ .

    Critics, however, argued that underdevelopment (4)_____ by capitalist development itself in the industrialised countries. Within a historical context, most of the LDCs (5)_____ by the developed nations. Colonialism (6)_____ to be the result of capitalism.

    When industrialism appeared in Europe, an international division of labour (7)_____ . Primary products (8)_____ to the industrialised countries by the colonies. These colonies, in turn, became the markets for the goods that (9)_____ and exported by the metropolitan powers.

Stage 2 Dependency theory

Comprehension

Pre-questions

Before you read the passage, read the following questions. Do you know the answers already? Discuss them with other students to see if they know the answers. The questions will help to give a purpose to your reading; it is not necessary to write the answers.

1 What 'constructive effects' could there have been from colonialism for a country such as India?
2 What could be the main effect of capitalist influence and control in LDCs?
3 Do the orthodox theories of economic backwardness and poverty seem to be satisfactory?

---

1   The vigorous outward thrust of the rapidly growing and changing societies of Western Europe incorporated large areas of the world into their spheres of interest. New patterns of production and trade were introduced, along with more advanced technical, scientific and infrastructural facilities. New
5   cultural and religious values and institutions were also introduced, but at the same time, old, established social and political structures, cultures and values were partially or totally destroyed and the processes of change that were occurring within the colonised societies were retarded and/or distorted.
10   Karl Marx, in his writings on the impact of British rule on India (Marx, 1853; 1973) emphasised the contradictory effects of colonialism – the destruction of the old society and economy coupled with the laying of the material foundations of Western society in Asia. Marx believed that in the long run the constructive effects of colonialism would outweigh the
15   destructive. Colonialism brought political unification, the establishment of private property in land, the creation of an Indian managerial and

entrepreneurial class and the possibility of the development of 'fresh productive powers' (through, for example, the development of railways). For Marx: 'the country that is more developed industrially only shows, to
20 the less developed, the image of its own future' (quoted in Palma, 1978, p. 889).

Clearly, Marx's predictions concerning India have yet to be fully realised. This apparent failure of the LDCs in general to develop rapidly and autonomously within a capitalist framework has given rise to a school of
25 thought called 'neo[1]-Marxism', which is concerned with the elaboration of a variety of theories of underdevelopment and dependency. For these theorists, the study of the development of the LDCs must give rise to a theory of dependence complementary to the theory of imperialism which evolved from the study of capitalist development in the metropolitan
30 centres (Dos Santos, 1973).

Paul Baran (Baran, 1957) is seen by many as the 'founder' of neo-Marxism. He argued that capitalist penetration of the LDCs developed some of the prerequisites of capitalist development but blocked others, largely through the removal of the previously accumulated and currently
35 generated economic surplus, which retarded capital accumulation, and through the destruction of indigenous industries. Capitalist development was 'distorted' to suit the purposes of Western imperialism and the LDCs were ruled by 'comprador bourgeoisies' (ruling classes) whose position was dependent on and allied to foreign interests. André Gunder Frank (1967)
40 has extended Baran's work, and has argued that there are processes at work within the world economy through which capitalist contradictions and capitalist development generated underdevelopment in the peripheral economies, whose surplus is expropriated, whilst generating development within the metropolitan centres that appropriate the surplus.

45 Frank's ideas have been extremely influential but increasingly criticised. His pursuit of a general theory of underdevelopment has tended to obscure the diversity of economic structure and experience found in the 'third world'. Others (for example, Cardoso and Faletto, 1979) have argued that a process of dependent development is occurring within a number of LDCs
50 such as Brazil, Mexico, India and Argentina. A process of 'internal structural fragmentation' is occurring within such countries, linking their most advanced sectors to the international capitalist system and turning their backward economic and social sectors into 'internal colonies'. However, such writers are no longer attempting to outline a general theory
55 of 'dependent capitalist development' but are more concerned with the identification and analysis of 'situations' of dependency. Such 'situations' are not necessarily either stable or permanent, and the social scientist must examine both the mechanisms that perpetuate 'situations' of dependency and the mechanisms at work within the system that bring about change.

60 Warren (1980, Ch. 7) has perhaps been the most vociferous of the critics of dependency theory. He argues that dependency theory is static in the sense that dependency is defined as given, with only its forms changing. He also criticises the assumptions made by many dependency theorists that

there existed a 'latent, suppressed historical alternative' to the development
65 that actually took place in the LDCs and that the failure of this alternative
development path to materialise was the result of external forces (colonialism). He maintains that it cannot be taken for granted that the social forces
capable of embodying the allegedly suppressed and superior alternative
actually existed and, more generally, he concludes that:

70   'The concept of dependence has always been imprecise; such significance as it
      has relates almost entirely to *political* control of one society by another. Since
      national economies are becoming increasingly *interdependent*, the meaning of
      dependence is ever more elusive, not to say mystical.'
                                                        (Warren, 1980, Ch. 7, p. 182)

75 We thus see that the orthodox explanations of economic backwardness
and poverty have been vigorously challenged in the past few years. There is,
as yet, however, no generally accepted radical explanation of the origins
and current forms of international inequality and underdevelopment.

---

[1]neo – a new or modern form or development of

References

Baran, P. (1957; 1973), *The Political Economy of Growth*, New York, Monthly Review Press; Harmondsworth, Penguin Books.

Cardoso, F. H. & Faletto, E. (1979), *Dependency and Development in Latin America*, Berkeley & Los Angeles, University of California Press.

Dos Santos, T. (1973), 'The Crisis of Development Theory and the Problem of Dependence in Latin America', in Bernstein, H. (ed.), *Underdevelopment and Development,* Harmondsworth, Penguin Books.

Frank, A. G. (1967), *Capitalism and Underdevelopment in Latin America*, New York, Monthly Review Press.

Marx, K. (1853; 1973), 'The East India Company – Its History and Results' and 'The Future Results of the British Rule in India', in Fernbach, D. (ed.) (1973), Karl Marx, *Surveys from Exile*, Political Writings, Vol. 2, Harmondsworth, Penguin Books.

Palma, G. (1978), 'Dependency: A Formal Theory of Underdevelopment or a Methodology for the Analysis of Concrete Situations of Underdevelopment?', *World Development*, Vol. 6, No. 7/8, July/August.

Rostow, W. W. (1962), *The Stages of Economic Growth: A Non-Communist Manifesto*, Cambridge University Press.

Szentes, T. (1971), *The Political Economy of Underdevelopment*, Budapest, Akademiai Kiado.

Warren, Bill (1980), *Imperialism: Pioneer of Capitalism*, London, Verso.

Comprehension

Post-questions

After you have read the passage write brief answers to the following questions. Try to express your answers in your own words if possible.

1 What were the 'contradictory effects of colonialism' referred to by Marx?
2 What would neo-Marxists expect of a study of the development of LDCs?
3 According to Frank, how have the Western imperialist countries benefited from their contact with LDCs?
4 According to some economists, what is the process of 'internal structural fragmentation' that is occurring within a number of LDCs?
5 What seem to be the two major criticisms of dependency theory, at least as seen by Warren?

Word study

**Exercise 1A
Alternative vocabulary**

Below is a list of words (and line numbers) from the text (1–24). Next to them is a list of synonyms (words or phrases with the same meaning) or explanations, in mixed order (a–x). Match the words from the text with their synonyms.

1	distorted (8)	a	loudest, most forceful
2	outweigh (14)	b	associated with and additional to
3	autonomously (24)	c	difficult to find
4	elaboration (25)	d	hide
5	complementary to (28)	e	become more important than
		f	twisted or altered
6	prerequisite (33)	g	existing but hidden
7	indigenous (36)	h	detailed expansion or development
8	allied to (39)	i	connected with, or linked to
9	peripheral (42)	j	a precondition or requirement for
10	expropriated (43)	k	taken way
11	appropriate (44)	l	internal or local
12	obscure (46)	m	separation into small parts
13	diversity (47)	n	containing or including
14	fragmentation (51)	o	located away from the centre; outer; on the fringe or edge
15	perpetuate (58)	p	assume as true, or accept as a fact
16	bring about (59)	q	independently
17	vociferous (60)	r	inexact
18	latent (64)	s	take for their own use
19	materialise (66)	t	supposedly
20	take for granted (67)	u	actually happen, become fact
21	embodying (68)	v	preserve, keep
22	allegedly (68)	w	variety
23	imprecise (70)	x	cause to happen
24	elusive (73)		

**Exercise 1B
Explanation**

The following words are taken from the text (line numbers are given). Can you explain their meaning as used in the text? Use a dictionary if necessary.

1 infrastructure (4)   4 accumulated (34)
2 entrepreneur (17)   5 static (61)
3 blocked (33)

**Exercise 2
Negative prefixes (1)**

A   In the texts in Units 1 and 2 there are a number of adjectives and adverbs that can be made negative by the addition of a prefix e.g. *productive – unproductive*. The prefix *un-* has the meaning of 'not' or 'the opposite of'. Another negative prefix is *in-* e.g. *equality – inequality*.

The words below are divided into those that are used with the prefix *un-* and those with *in-*. Write down the prefixed words.

1 **un-**	productive	orthodox	2 **in-**	equality
	acceptable	profitable		accurate
	certain	satisfactory		definite
	changed	stable		dependent
	developed	successful		direct
	economic			distinct
	employment			efficient
	equal			formally
	important			significant
	necessary			sufficient

Note: Both adjective and adverb forms of the words in the first list take the same prefix e.g. *unproductive*, *unproductively*.

B The prefix *in-* changes to combine with the letter that follows it:
a *in-* becomes *il-* before *l*: e.g. *logical – illogical*
b *in-* becomes *im-* before *b, m, p*: e.g. *possibility – impossibility*
c *in-* becomes *ir-* before *r*: e.g. *religious – irreligious*.

Decide which prefix (*il-, im-, ir-*) each of the following words should have and write down its correct negative form. Make tables like the ones of words with *un-* and *in-* above.

balance	moral	personal	regular	patient
legible	replaceable	permanent	legitimate	mobility
legal	responsible	relevant	perfect	
literate	precise	mature		

C In addition to the prefixes shown above, there are three others that are sometimes used to indicate the negative, or opposite, or 'without'.
a *non-* e.g. *non-contributory, non-equivalent, non-monetary*
b *dis-* e.g. *disequilibrium, dishonest, dissatisfaction, dissimilar*
c *a-* There is a very small group of words that uses this prefix; the main ones are as follows: *ahistorical, amoral, apolitical, asocial, asymmetrical, atypical.*

Exercise 3
Negative prefixes (2)

Rewrite the following sentences to give them a negative or opposite meaning by using the correct prefix with the appropriate adjective or adverb.
e.g. His arguments about development theory were very *logical*.
His arguments about development theory were very *illogical*.

1 Projections of economic growth are generally accurate.
2 In many ways, using GNP *per capita* as an indicator of economic welfare is satisfactory.
3 The mobility of labour is a factor to consider in economic development.
4 Initially, development economics was a distinct area of study.
5 Some of the early theories of economic development are relevant today.

Open exercise

You could add to your tables of prefixes any negative-meaning adjectives/adverbs that you find in later units. In this way you can provide yourself with a useful reference list of such words that are suitable for use in economics writing.

Exercise 4
Formation of adjectives

In the text in Stages 1 and 2 of this unit there are a number of adjectives that end in *-al*. This exercise gives practice in forming adjectives ending in *-al* from nouns; it also gives practice in producing nouns from the adjectives. e.g. *infrastructure* (noun) – *infrastructural* (adjective)
technology (noun) – *technological* (adjective)

1 Write down the adjective that is formed from each of these nouns.

structure	history	manager	periphery
culture	mystique	entrepreneur	theory

2 Now write down the nouns from which these adjectives are formed.

colonial	national	social
industrial	influential	political

Check carefully in the texts how these adjectives are used.

Language use

Exercise 1
Reference skills (1)

The references to books and journals after the Stage 2 passage are arranged in alphabetical order (A–Z) of the author's surname. If more than one reference by the same author is given, then the earlier dated reference appears first.[1]

The nine references from the passage (labelled A–I) are in the correct order: they are reproduced below. Now add to them the eleven references given below them (labelled J–T). Re-arrange them all so that they are in the correct order (alphabetical and date). Indicate the correct order by numbering the letter labels (A–T) from 1 to 20: e.g. 1T.

Dependency theory: references

A Baran, P. (1957; 1973), *The Political Economy of Growth*, New York, Monthly Review Press; Harmondsworth, Penguin Books.

B Cardoso, F. H. & Faletto, E. (1979), *Dependency and Development in Latin America*, Berkeley & Los Angeles, University of California Press.

C Dos Santos, T. (1973), 'The Crisis of Development Theory and the Problem of Dependence in Latin America', in Bernstein, H. (ed.), *Underdevelopment and Development*, Harmondsworth, Penguin Books.

D Frank, A. G. (1967), *Capitalism and Underdevelopment in Latin America*, New York, Monthly Review Press.

E Marx, K. (1853; 1973), 'The East India Company – Its History and Results' and 'The Future Results of the British Rule in India', in Fernbach, D. (ed.) (1973), Karl Marx, *Surveys from Exile*, Political Writings, Vol. 2, Harmondsworth, Penguin Books.

F Palma, G. (1978), 'Dependency: A Formal Theory of Underdevelopment or a Methodology for the Analysis of Concrete Situations of Underdevelopment?', *World Development*, Vol. 6, No. 7/8, July/August.

G Rostow, W. W. (1962), *The Stages of Economic Growth: A Non-Communist Manifesto*, Cambridge University Press.

H Szentes, T. (1971), *The Political Economy of Underdevelopment*, Budapest, Akademiai Kiado.

I Warren, Bill (1980), *Imperialism: Pioneer of Capitalism*, London, Verso.

Additional bibliographical references

J Amin, S. (1976), *Unequal Development: An Essay on the Social Formation of Peripheral Capitalism*, Hassocks, Harvester Press.

K Frank, A. G. (1977), 'Dependence is Dead: Long Live Dependence and the Class Struggle: An Answer to Critics', *World Development*, Vol. 5, No. 4, pp. 355–370.

L Lall, S. (1975), 'Is "Dependence" a Useful Concept in Analysing Underdevelopment?', *World Development*, Vol. 3, No. 11 & 12, pp. 799–810.

M Foster-Carter, A. (1974), 'Neo-Marxist Approaches to Development and Underdevelopment', in de Kadt, E. and Williams, G. (eds.), *Sociology and Development*, London, Tavistock.

N Schiffer, J. (1981), 'The Changing Post-War Pattern of Development: The Accumulated Wisdom of Samir Amin', *World Development*, Vol. 9, No. 6, pp. 515–537.

---

[1]See Appendix 1: Study skills (C Referencing).

O Warren, Bill (1973), 'Imperialism and Capitalist Industrialisation', *New Left Review*, No. 81, September–October, pp. 3–44.

P Cardoso, F. H. (1972), 'Dependent-Capitalist Development in Latin America', *New Left Review*, No. 74, July–August, pp. 83–95.

Q Leys, C. (1975), *Underdevelopment in Kenya: The Political Economy of Neo-Colonialism*. London, Heinemann.

R Brewer, A. (1982), *Marxist Theories of Imperialism*, London, Routledge & Kegan Paul.

S Smith, Sheila (1982), 'Class Analysis versus World Systems: Critique of Samir Amin's Typology of Under-Development', *Journal of Contemporary Asia*, Vol. 12, No. 1, pp. 7–18; reprinted in Limquecoe, P. and McFarlane, B. (eds.), *Neo-Marxist Theories of Development*, London, Croom Helm.

T Amin, S. (1974), 'Accumulation and Development: A Theoretical Model', *Review of African Political Economy*, No. 1, August–November, pp. 9–26.

Exercise 2
Reference skills (2)

The following are examination-type or essay questions. Read them carefully and then decide which references, from the twenty listed above, would seem to be appropriate reading to help in answering the questions. For each question write the letter-labels (A–T) of the appropriate references. (Do *not* answer the questions themselves).

For example, if the question was 'Briefly outline André Gunder Frank's theory of the "development of underdevelopment".', then we might choose A. G. Frank's book and article – references D and K.

1 Critically evaluate Samir Amin's concept of 'Unequal Development'.

2 Outline the various theories of dependency that have influenced, in recent years, the way in which economists have analysed development and underdevelopment. How useful do you find such theories in analysing and understanding the problems faced by the less developed countries?

3 In what ways do 'structuralist' or 'neo-Marxist' interpretations of recent Latin American economic development differ from more orthodox analyses?

Exercise 3
Summary

The following passage is a summary of the Stage 2 text 'Dependency theory'. Complete the summary by writing down one word for each numbered space. The first one has been done as an example. Read the passage through quickly before writing anything. Try not to look back at the text again.

The rapid growth of <u>Western Europe</u> brought many parts of the world into its field of influence. New economic patterns and cultural values were introduced, and the old ones were changed or destroyed.
   (1)_____ (2)_____ stressed the opposing effects of (3)_____: the destruction of the old way of life contrasted with the introduction of new business ventures and practices. He thought that in the long run the advantages of colonialism would become more important than the disadvantages, especially regarding industrial development.
   Because LDCs seem to have failed to develop rapidly and independently within a capitalist (4)_____, (5)_____ has arisen. It is concerned with developing a theory of dependence relevant to LDCs.

Probably the first neo-Marxist was (6)_____ (7)_____ , who argued that the main effect of foreign capitalism in LDCs was to remove any economic (8)_____ . André Gunder Frank has extended Baran's work. He has argued that the removal of the economic surplus from the colonies has caused them to become (9)_____ , while at the same time it has helped the Western industrialised countries to develop.

Frank's ideas have been criticised. Other writers have argued that a process of (10)_____ development is occurring within a number of LDCs. This process involves the division of LDCs' economies into advanced (11)_____ , which are linked to the international capitalist system, and the backward sectors, which become 'internal colonies'. Such critics are largely concerned with analysing 'situations' of (12)_____.

(13)_____ has been the most forceful (14)_____ of dependency theory. He argues that dependency theory is (15)_____ in that it assumes that the condition of dependency is given, with only its (16)_____ changing. He also criticises the assumptions that are often made, saying it should not be assumed that alternative development was possible for (17)_____.

Although there has been dissatisfaction with conventional theories of underdevelopment, there is as yet no generally new theory to take their place.

Extension activities

1 Writing: Essay

Outline the various theories of dependency that have influenced, in recent years, the way in which economists have analysed development and underdevelopment. (See the notes in the Key for some useful information on writing the introduction to this essay.)

2 Group activity: Pairwork – questions

1 After brief discussion with a partner, compose and write down a suitable question about each of the writers referred to in the text, *viz*.

Karl Marx	André Gunder Frank
Paul Baran	Bill Warren

Make sure that the question you compose can be answered from the information in the text.

When you have finished, ask another pair your questions (you and your partner can ask two questions each). Decide if their answers are correct. Then the other pair can ask you questions in the same way.

2 Look carefully at the four quotations which follow. All of them are taken from the text. With your partner compose a suitable question for each (making sure that it can be answered from the text), and in the same way as 1 above ask the questions of another pair.

   a 'the country that is more developed industrially only shows, to the less developed, the image of its own future' (19)

   b 'capitalist penetration of the LDCs developed some of the prerequisites of capitalist development' (32)

   c 'capitalist contradictions and capitalist development generated underdevelopment in the peripheral economies' (41)

   d 'the meaning of dependence is ever more elusive' (73)

Note: See the notes in the Key for examples of questions.
If you have difficulty in forming questions see Language use Exercise 1: Question forms, in Unit 8 Stage 1.

Unit 3   Economics for development

Stage 1   The relevance of Western economics?

1   For a quarter of a century, economists have argued over the relevance and usefulness of 'Western' economics to 'non-Western' economies.

The debate was largely initiated by Dudley Seers in 1963 with the publication of his article entitled 'The Limitations of the Special Case'. The
5   'special case' was the private-enterprise, developed industrial economy, characterised by Seers as 'an autonomous and flexible socio-economic structure, in which each human being responds individually to the material incentives offered and which is subject to no formidable exogenous strains' (Seers, 1963, p. 83).
10   Seers conceded that certain elementary propositions retained their general validity in the context of LDCs, but he was particularly critical of the application of macro-economic concepts and models. He argued that propositions derived from largely static analysis were irrelevant and perhaps misleading, and that insufficient attention had been paid to the
15   specific political and institutional structures of the LDCs. Most importantly, the study of the LDCs could not be divorced from an examination of their position within the world economy, not least because of the 'openness' of their economies, their dependence on the developed industrial economies as markets for their (mainly) primary product exports and their vulner-
20   ability to protective measures imposed by such economies.

Paul Streeten (1967) further refined and strengthened the critique of orthodox economic theory. He argued that economic models, particularly those used in development planning, were subject to a number of related and systematic biases, *viz*:
25   1 the separation of parameters (social and legal institutions, psychological attitudes) from variables; this might be appropriate and justifiable in Western economies, but in LDCs a simple distinction should not be made between 'economic' and 'non-economic' factors;

2 the tendency to select one factor (for example, capital or education) as
30   *the* strategic factor in development;

3 the tendency to assign the role of *sufficient* condition to what may or may not be one of several *necessary* conditions for development;

4 the failure to recognise that many concepts formed by aggregation ('income', 'employment', 'savings', 'investment') are often based on
35   implicit value judgements and presuppose the existence of conditions that might well be absent in LDCs (see for example the discussion of the concepts of 'employment' and 'unemployment' in Unit 5, Stage 2).[1]

---

[1] Streeten refers to these four points as, respectively:
  a *adapted ceteris paribus* or *automatic mutatis mutandis*

b one factor analysis   **c** illegitimate isolation   **d** misplaced aggregation.
It should be noted that Streeten was not only criticising neo-classical economic theory
and that his strictures were against the economics profession as a whole. Seers, too, aimed
at a wide target – he was critical of much (Soviet) Marxist writing on development problems.

Comprehension

A   The following statements are based upon the information in the passage. If a statement is correct, write T (TRUE); if it is wrong, write F (FALSE).

1 Dudley Seers really started the arguments that have been going on for twenty-five years about the relevance of Western economics to non-Western economies.

2 Although Seers admitted that some fundamental concepts were generally appropriate for LDCs, he found fault with the application of macro-economics to LDCs.

3 According to Seers the 'openness' of LDCs' economies was not a reason for looking at their position in the world economy.

4 Paul Streeten also criticised conventional economic theory by arguing that economic models were likely to have several biases.

5 In reality there may be a number of necessary conditions for development, yet there is a tendency to allot the role of the only sufficient condition to merely one of them.

B   Write brief answers to the following questions, obtaining your information from the passage.

1 According to Dudley Seers, what was the 'special case'?
2 Why was Seers not in favour of using static analysis for LDCs?
3 According to Seers, what was the significance of the LDCs' position in the world economy?
4 In Streeten's view, was it appropriate to choose one factor as being crucial for development?

Word study

Exercise 1A
Alternative vocabulary

The following words and phrases could be used in place of some of those in the text. They also explain the meaning of those words. For each word/phrase below write down the word/phrase in the text that it could replace. Also write the line number. Use a dictionary if necessary.

1 originated, started
2 extremely difficult to overcome
3 external
4 admitted
5 obtained, got
6 separated from
7 weakness when faced with
8 tending or likely to have, prone to
9 tendencies
10 limiting factors
11 items which may vary
12 allot, allocate
13 assume, imply

Exercise 1B
Explanation

The following phrases are taken from the text (line numbers are given). Can you explain their meaning as used in the text? Use a dictionary if necessary.

1 open economy (17)
2 primary products (19)
3 aggregation (33)

Exercise 2
Past tense forms

From reading the texts so far in the book, and from doing some of the exercises, you will have noticed that the **past simple active tense** (e.g. *he believed*) and the **past simple passive** (e.g. *it was introduced*) are commonly used in economics writing.

For the majority of verbs, the regular verbs, these tenses are formed by adding either *-ed* or *-d* to the infinitive of the verb e.g. *attempt – attempted*, *argue – argued*. Note that some verbs double the last letter before adding *-ed* e.g. *occur – occurred*, *prefer – preferred*, *permit – permitted*, *fit – fitted* (*but benefit – benefited*), *signal – signalled*, *travel – travelled*.

For many verbs ending in *-y* e.g. *deny* (*he denies* = present tense), the past tense is formed by changing the *-y* to *i* and adding *-ed* e.g. *he denied*.

1 Write out the past tense forms of the verbs below.

  a deny   **d** imply
  b ally   **e** reply
  c identify   **f** study

2 The following verbs have been taken from the texts in the first three units of this book. They all have irregular forms for the past simple tense and the past participle (which is used to form the past simple passive). Write down as many past simple tense forms and past participles as you can, then carefully check the answers. Here is an example:

  verb infinitive   *past simple tense*   *past participle*
  become   became   become

  a break   **f** lead   **k** pay
  b bring   **g** leave   **l** see
  c find   **h** make   **m** take
  d give   **i** mean   **n** underlie
  e hide   **j** overcome

Language use

Exercise 1
Prepositions

The following is a shortened form of the Stage 1 text. Write down a suitable preposition (words like *in*, *at*, *for*, etc.) for each numbered space. Think carefully about the meaning of a whole sentence before you write anything. Do not look back at the Stage 1 text unless you have great difficulty.

(1)_____ a long time, economists have argued (2)_____ the relevance (3)_____ Western economics (4)_____ non-Western economies.
   The debate was started (5)_____ Dudley Seers (6)_____ 1963 (7)_____ the publication (8)_____ his article entitled 'The Limitations (9)_____ the Special Case'.
   Seers admitted that certain fundamental propositions retained their general validity (10)_____ the context (11)_____ LDCs, but he was

especially critical (12)_____ the application (13)_____ macro-economics. He argued that not enough attention has been paid (14)_____ the specific structures (15)_____ the LDCs. (16)_____ particular, the study (17)_____ the LDCs could not be separated (18)_____ an examination (19)_____ their position (20)_____ the world economy. It was important to remember the 'openness' (21)_____ their economies, their dependence (22)_____ the developed countries as markets (23)_____ their exports, and their vulnerability (24)_____ protective measures imposed (25)_____ such economies.

Exercise 2
The structure of narration

Narration, or the describing of events in order, frequently makes use of verbs in the past simple tense – both active and passive. Look at the structure of the Stage 1 text below.

Paragraph 1	Over a period of time (until now), economists *have argued* . . .	*Commentary* present perfect active
Paragraph 2	The debate *was initiated* by Seers . . . . . . his article (which *was*) *entitled* . . . . . . economy (which *was*) *characterised* by Seers . . . . . . material incentives (which *are*) *offered* . . .	past simple passive reduced relative clause and past simple passive reduced relative clause and past simple passive reduced relative clause and present simple passive
Paragraph 3	Seers *conceded* that . . . He *argued* that . . . . . . propositions (which *were*) *derived* from . . . . . . insufficient attention *had been paid* to . . . . . . protective measures (which *were*) *imposed* by . . .	past simple active past simple active reduced relative clause and past simple passive past perfect passive reduced relative clause and past simple passive
Paragraph 4	Streeten *refined* and *strengthened* . . . He *argued* that . . .	past simple active past simple active

Note:
1 Paragraph 1 is an introductory statement summarising what follows.
2 Practice is given in using passives in Unit 2 Stage 1 Language use exercises.
3 Information on reduced relative clauses is given in Unit 1 Stage 2 Language use exercise 2 (p. 19).

Now try to write a brief summary of the text in Unit 2 Stage 2. Look back at the text and model your summary upon the structure shown here. Write one or two sentences as an introductory statement; divide your summary into paragraphs and, as far as possible, use the past simple active and passive tenses.

Stage 2 Economics or development economics?

Comprehension

Pre-questions

Before you read the passage, read the following questions. Do you know the answers already? Discuss them with other students to see if they know the answers. The questions will help to give a purpose to your reading; it is not necessary to write the answers.

1 Should the scarce resources in LDCs be allocated through the use of the price mechanism?
2 What is social cost–benefit analysis?
3 What part can macro-economics play in theorising about the economic development of LDCs?

1   Streeten emphasised that he was not rejecting all analytical or planning models.

> 'Rigorous abstraction, simplification and quantification are necessary conditions of analysis and policy. But models must be realistic, relevant and
5 useful. The trouble with many current models is that they are shapely and elegant, but lack the vital organs.'

(Streeten, 1967, p. 57)

Although Seers, Streeten and other like-minded economists mounted a powerful and sustained onslaught on orthodox economics, both neo-
10 classical and Keynesian, the established orthodoxy was by no means defeated. The defenders of the neo-classical paradigm, such as Myint (1967) and Bauer (1971) continued to argue that the orthodox static theory of the allocation of scarce resources was as relevant to the less developed as to the developed economies, and that the market remained the most efficient and
15 effective mechanism for the proper allocation of those scarce resources.

In a more recent work in the neo-classical tradition, Little (1982, Ch. 2) has elaborated on the distinction that is made between 'structuralist' and neo-classical economics. Structuralists, he argues, see the world as inflexible, with change inhibited by a variety of obstacles, bottlenecks, rigidities
20 and constraints. They thus distrust the price mechanism and seek to promote change in other ways. The neo-classical view of the world, on the other hand, is one of flexibility. The price mechanism is expected to work rather well, and neo-classical economics can be described as

> '.... a paradigm that tells one to investigate markets and prices, perhaps
25 expecting them often to work well, but also to be on the watch for aberrations and ways of correcting them. Perhaps the single best touchstone is a concern for prices and their role.'

(Little, 1982, pp. 25–6)

To support their arguments, neo-classical economists point to the success
30 that a number of LDCs have had in recent years in breaking into export markets for manufactured goods through the implementation of policies conducive to export promotion (see Unit 6). They also argue that empirical evidence is increasingly becoming available that supports the neo-classical contention that, if factor prices are 'right' (that is, if they reflect their social
35 opportunity cost), firms will substitute cheaper labour for more expensive

capital and thus create greater employment opportunities through the use of more labour-intensive techniques of production (see Unit 8).

Perhaps the main achievement of the neo-classical school, however, has been the development of the techniques of social cost–benefit analysis 40 (SCB). This is a technique of project evaluation designed to ensure that projects are selected according to their *social* profitability. Because market prices are likely to be 'distorted', shadow prices are estimated with which social costs and benefits are calculated, and social welfare is maximised by maximising the net present value of the stream of benefits, net of costs, 45 using an appropriate discount rate.

SCB has been widely used by international agencies and national planning ministries.[1] It has not, however, escaped criticism, and economists such as Stewart (1975) and Lall (1976) have attacked both the methodology of SCB and the basic principles which underlie it. Lall in particular has 50 criticised what he conceives to be the ideological base of welfare economics (the assumption of a harmony of interests between all members of society), its individualistic premises (its ignoring the formation of preferences) and its state power premises (that the state is neutral, that it acts in the 'national interest', etc.).

55 SCB is an application of neo-classical micro-economic analysis. As was noted in Stage 1, however, Seers (1963) also criticised the application of orthodox Keynesian macro-economics to LDCs. Macro-economics is concerned with the economy as a whole in terms of aggregate variables and focuses on the determinants of aggregate supply and demand for national 60 output. Perhaps in this area more than in any other, there was general agreement in the literature that Keynesian short-run demand management analysis was not relevant to the problems faced by LDCs and as a consequence there was, until recently, little discussion of issues relating to short- and medium-term macro-economic management in LDCs (Little, 65 1982, p. x). The main area of controversy in the macro-economic field was the conflict between 'structuralists' and 'monetarists' over the causes of, and cures for, inflation, a debate that is considered in greater detail in Unit 10, Stage 2.

More recently, a structuralist macro-economic theory has begun to 70 emerge. Taylor (1983, p. 3) argues that

'An economy has structure if its institutions and the behaviour of its members make some patterns of resource allocation and evolution substantially more likely than others. Economic analysis is structuralist when it takes these factors as the foundation stones for its theories.'

75 The attempt to incorporate the specific structural features of LDCs into macro-economic theory represents an important advance in the continued evolution of 'development economics'. Many would still argue, however, that 'economics is not enough', and that what is needed is a move towards explicitly multi-disciplinary 'development studies'.

80 The emergence of 'development studies' will not lead to the disappearance of the individual disciplines within the social sciences, but will rather create the opportunities for the breaking down of the barriers between

those disciplines and the encouragement of greater communication between the various development specialists in economics, politics, sociology,
85 anthropology, economic history, and so on. It is to be hoped that a more complete understanding of the problems of poverty and inequality, at both the national and international level, will emerge from this broader, multi-disciplinary approach and that policy prescriptions can be made more relevant and realistic.

---

[1]The use of SCB by development planners has largely been directed towards trying to make the market work more efficiently as an allocator of resources, rather than replacing the market through more direct, interventionist, economic planning.

References

Bauer, P. (1971), *Dissent on Development*, London, Weidenfeld and Nicolson.

Lall, S. (1976), 'Conflicts and Concepts: Welfare Economics and Developing Countries', *World Development*, Vol. 4, No. 3, March, pp. 181–95.

Little, I. M. D. (1982), *Economic Development: Theory, Policy and International Relations*, New York, Basic Books.

Myint, H. (1967), 'Economic Theory and the Underdeveloped Countries', in Martin, K., and Knapp, J. (eds.), *The Teaching of Development Economics*, London, Frank Cass, pp. 33–52.

Seers, D. (1963), 'The Limitations of the Special Case', *Bulletin of the Oxford University Institute of Economics and Statistics*, Vol. 25, No. 2, May, pp. 77–98.

Stewart, F. (1975), 'A Note on Social Cost–Benefit Analysis and Class Conflict in LDCs', *World Development*, Vol. 3, No. 1, January, pp. 31–39.

Streeten, P. (1967), 'The Use and Abuse of Models in Development Planning', in Martin K., and Knapp, J. (eds.), *The Teaching of Development Economics*, London, Frank Cass, pp. 57–83.

Taylor, L. (1983), *Structuralist Macroeconomics*, New York, Basic Books.

Comprehension

Post-questions

After you have read the passage write brief answers to the following questions. Try to express your answers in your own words if possible.

1 What was Streeten's main criticism of some planning models?
2 What is Little's view of the role of the price mechanism?
3 What evidence is there to support the neo-classical view of the role of prices?
4 How useful was Keynesian macro-economics thought to be for LDCs?
5 What would seem to be the advantages of the creation of 'development studies'?

Word study

Exercise 1A
Alternative vocabulary

Below is a list of words (and line numbers) from the text (1–19). Next to them is a list of synonyms or explanations, in mixed order (a–s). Match the words from the text with their synonyms.

1 rigorous (3)	a a test or criterion for determining the quality or genuineness of something
2 quantification (3)	b dispute, argument, debate
3 onslaught (9)	c directive
4 paradigm (11)	d statement on which reasoning is based
5 mechanism (15)	e attack
6 inflexible (18)	f model
7 inhibited (19)	

8 bottleneck (19)	g a blockage causing a slowing down
9 constraint (20)	h deviation from the norm
10 aberration (25)	i structure or arrangement
11 touchstone (26)	j form the basis of
12 conducive to (32)	k likely to encourage, contributing to
13 contention (34)	l strict and accurate
14 underlie (49)	m measurement
15 premise (52)	n instead
16 controversy (65)	o prevented, hindered
17 substantially (72)	p considerably
18 rather (81)	q limitations, restrictions
19 prescription (88)	r assertion, argument
	s rigid, fixed

Exercise 1B
Explanation

The following phrases are taken from the text (line numbers are given). Can you explain their meaning? Use a dictionary if necessary.

1 empirical evidence (32)   **3** labour-intensive techniques
2 shadow price (42)   of production (37)

Language use

Exercise 1
Verb tense: present simple

In using the present simple active tense, students often make a mistake by omitting the final -*s* from the third person singular ending e.g. *he thinks* (but: *they think*).

The following passage has been taken from the text and modified. Complete the passage by writing down an appropriate verb from the list for each numbered space. Write the appropriate form of the verb (singular or plural). Use each verb only once. The first verb has been done for you.

   argue, believe, distrust, encourage, exist, give, point out, seek, support, view, work

Structuralists ___*see*___ the world as inflexible, Little (1)_____ . They (2)_____ the price mechanism and (3)_____ to promote change in other ways. Neo-classicists, on the other hand, (4)_____ the world as being flexible. They (5)_____ that the price mechanism (6)_____ rather well. Neo-classicists (7)_____ their arguments by pointing to the success that a number of LDCs have had recently through the implementation of policies that (8)_____ the export promotion of manufactured goods. They also (9)_____ that empirical evidence (10)_____ which (11)_____ support to their view.

Exercise 2
Negatives

A   In these first three units in the book the negative has been expressed in a number of ways. Let us look at some examples:
a it will *not* lead to . . .
b it does *not* solve . . .
c there is *no* generally accepted radical explanation . . .
In (a), where verb tenses contain an auxiliary verb (e.g. *will*), *not* is placed after the auxiliary e.g.
They have not been able to overcome . . . ,
or after the verbs *be* and *have* if they are full verbs.

In (b), where a verb tense does not contain an auxiliary, *do, does, did* + *not* + verb infinitive (without *to*) is used e.g.
He agreed – He did not agree.

In (c), *no* can be used as an adjective e.g.
He had no answer.

Note: The phrase *by no means* = not at all, on no account, in no way.

B   Let us look at some other examples:

unless it is explicitly assumed . . . = *if . . . not*
to judge *whether or not* it is taking place . . . = *if . . . or not*
X was seen, *not* as Y, *but* as Z = instead of (an alternative is proposed)
. . . not only . . . (but also . . .) = something additional

The negative can also be expressed by:
none – used as a pronoun e.g. They had none.
neither . . . (nor . . .) = not one nor the other, of two, e.g. Neither theory is
acceptable.
Neither this theory nor that theory is acceptable.

Note: Certain verbs include a negative within their meaning e.g.
to lack = to not have, to be without
to deny = to say that something is not true
to refuse = not to accept or do or give

1 Complete the following paragraph, which has been adapted from the
   Stage 2 text, by writing down an appropriate negative form for each
   numbered space. Keep more or less the same meaning as in the original
   text.

   Streeten stressed that he rejected (1)_____ all the analytical (2)_____
   all the planning models. However, he emphasised that models should be
   (3)_____ rigorous (4)_____ realistic. If a model had (5)_____
   relevance, then it was (6)_____ useful. He considered that many current
   models (7)_____ have 'the vital organs'.

2 Using the information in A and B above, make the following sentence
   negative in four different ways, ensuring that both parts of the sentence
   have a negative meaning.
   If a model had relevance, then it was useful.

3 **Open question** Complete the following sentences in an appropriate way.
   a LDCs are often not only _____ but also _____ .
   b In many cases, LDCs have neither _____ nor _____ .
   c When discussing the causes of inflation there is often no . . .
   d Unless a theory . . .

Language use

Exercise 3
Summary: missing words

Below is a summary of the Stage 2 text. In each line one word (or an
abbreviation) has been deliberately omitted. Decide which word is missing
and where it should go. The missing word will never be the first or last
word on a line.
Here is an example: 1 . . . conventional *economic* theory . . .

1 Supporters of conventional theory, such as Myint
2 and, resisted attacks by arguing that the market
3 was the best for the allocation of scarce resources,
4 even LDCs.
5   Little, another neo-classical, tried to distinguish
6 between and neo-classical economics. According to

7 him, structuralists consider the world to be : they
8 prefer to cause change by means other than the mechanism.
9 The supporters, however, see the world as being flexible.
10 They prefer to use the price mechanism; in of it, they
11 give some evidence from a of LDCs.
12   The neo-classical has been responsible for developing
13 the of social cost–benefit analysis (SCB). Its purpose
14 is to make certain that are socially profitable. However,
15 some economists, notably Stewart and Lall, have both
16 the used by SCB and its underlying basic principles.
17   Until recently, there was little of macro-economic
18 theory relating to. However, now a structuralist macro-
19 economic theory is to appear which tries to include
20 particular features of LDCs. Many would argue that
21 although this is an, it does not go far enough, and
22 that what is needed is multi-disciplinary studies. It
23 is hoped that this would to a better understanding of
24 the problems of poverty and at all levels.

Extension activities

1 Writing: Essay

'For a quarter of a century, economists have argued over the relevance and usefulness of "Western" economics to "non-Western" economies.'
In your opinion have LDCs anything useful to learn from 'Western' industrialised economies?

2 Group activity: Pairwork and group work – discussion

a Making use of the Stage 2 text, in pairs discuss and list the main differences between neo-classical and structuralist economics. The views of a number of economists on the neo-classical and structuralist approaches are quoted or noted in the text. Discuss these and note which you consider to be the most significant comments or views. Compare your conclusions with other pairs.

b What are your own views on the neo-classical and structuralist approaches? Discuss these together in a group.

Unit 4   Poverty and inequality

Stage 1   Absolute poverty

1   The great majority of the population of LDCs live in conditions of abject poverty. A condition of absolute poverty is experienced when the income or consumption of a person or household falls below a normatively defined poverty line, 'a condition of life so characterised by malnutrition, illiteracy
5   and disease as to be beneath the reasonable definition of human decency' (World Bank, 1980, p. 32).

     It has been estimated (Chenery *et al.*, 1974, Ch. 1) that in 1969 there were 370 million people with a *per capita* income of US $50 or less, and 578 million people with a *per capita* income of US $75 or less.[1] By 1975 the
10   number of people in absolute poverty had risen to 780 million.[2]

     About one-half of the world's absolute poor live in South Asia (mainly India and Bangladesh), one-sixth live in East and Southeast Asia (mainly Indonesia) and a further one-sixth live in sub-Saharan Africa. The poor are disproportionately located in rural areas and a substantial proportion of
15   them are self-employed (the question of employment in LDCs is discussed in Unit 5) but suffer from very low income levels, partly because of their limited access to productive assets (especially agricultural land).

     Poverty lines can be defined either with reference to the estimated cost of a bundle of 'basic goods' at relevant prices, or with respect to a nutritional
20   norm, such as the 'required' intake of calories and proteins. Neither approach, however, is free from problems of definition and measurement. For example, the composition of the bundle of 'basic goods' is not independent of the socio-cultural characteristics of the population, the structure of the economy and climate. Calorie requirements vary according
25   to age, sex, climate and type of work performed, and there are complex and not fully understood interrelationships between nutrition, health, education and fertility which must be recognised for policy purposes (Srinivasan, 1977).

     There is thus always an arbitrary element in the definition of absolute
30   poverty: 'To be socially meaningful, minimum levels cannot be defined according to some absolute biological standards but must necessarily vary with the general level of economic, social and political development' (Chenery *et al.*, 1974, p. 11).

---

[1]The estimates of the absolute poor are for 44 countries representing approximately 60% of the total population of LDCs, excluding China, at 1971 prices.

[2]It should be noted that this figure was calculated in a different manner from the earlier ones, and was derived from detailed studies of poverty in India.

Comprehension

A   The following statements are based upon the information in the passage. If a statement is correct, write T (TRUE); if it is wrong, write F (FALSE).

1 Absolute poverty exists when *per capita* income falls below a certain, defined, very low level.
2 From 1969 to 1975 there was a decrease in the number of people living in absolute poverty.
3 Proportionately more poor people are to be found in country areas.
4 There are two ways to define poverty : neither presents any kind of problem.
5 Many would argue that poverty is only meaningful in a relative sense.

B   Write brief answers to the following questions, obtaining your information from the passage.

1 For 1969 two figures are shown for *per capita* income – US $50 and $75. Could both of them represent absolute poverty?
2 Give one reason why many self-employed people in rural areas have very low incomes.
3 What are some of the problems associated with using a nutritional norm in defining poverty?
4 Why is it not possible to have one satisfactory definition of absolute poverty?

Word study

Exercise 1A
Alternative vocabulary

Below is a list of words (and line numbers) from the text (1–11). Next to them is a list of synonyms or explanations, in mixed order (a–k). Match the words from the text with their synonyms.

1 abject (1)	a based on random selection, choice, or personal opinion, not on reason
2 absolute (2)	b units of energy supplied by food
3 malnutrition (4)	c package, collection
4 illiteracy (4)	d differ, are different
5 bundle (19)	e wretched, miserable, hopeless
6 norm (20)	f complex organic chemical compounds essential for good health, obtained in such foods as: meat, fish, cheese, eggs, milk
7 calories (20)	
8 proteins (20)	
9 vary (24)	g condition caused by inadequate food or lack of the right kind of food
10 fertility (27)	h standard
11 arbitrary (29)	i ability to produce young
	j complete
	k inability to read or write, lack of education

Exercise 1B
Explanation

The following phrases are taken from the text (line numbers are given). Can you explain their meaning as used in the text? Use a dictionary if necessary.

1 household (3)
2 sub-Saharan Africa (13)
3 The poor are disproportionately located in rural areas (13)
4 assets (17)
5 the 'required' intake (20)

**Exercise 2
Continents, regions, countries and currencies**

1 In addition to the two continents given below, name the other five:
Australia   Antarctica

2 Many countries are grouped into regions and are often referred to by those names in economics. Some of the regions are named below on the left. On the right is a list of countries in mixed order. Write down which countries belong to each group.

SCANDINAVIA
(a group of countries in Northern Europe)

THE MIDDLE EAST
(the countries in Asia west of India)

THE FAR EAST
(the countries in Asia east of India)

SOUTHEAST ASIA

LATIN AMERICA
(the Spanish and Portuguese-speaking countries of South and Central America)

SUB-SAHARAN AFRICA
(the countries in Africa south of the Sahara Desert)

Iraq	Iran
Niger	China
Mexico	Denmark
Burma	Brazil
Sudan	South Korea
North Korea	Mali
Indonesia	Norway
Sweden	Saudi Arabia
Thailand	Argentina
Egypt	Japan
Iceland	Malaysia
Chad	Peru

3 In the table below are three columns for the names of some countries, the adjectives formed from those names and the unit of currency used in those countries. What are the missing words?

Country	Adjective	Currency
Brazil	Brazilian	cruzeiro
China	_____	yuan
_____	Danish	krone
Egypt	_____	pound
France	_____	_____
Germany	_____	_____
_____	Greek	drachma
Hong Kong	_____	dollar
India	_____	_____
Iran	_____	rial
_____	Italian	lira
Japan	_____	_____
Kenya	_____	shilling
Malaysia	_____	ringgit
_____	Mexican	peso
Netherlands (Holland)	_____	guilder
Nigeria	_____	naira
Portugal	_____	escudo
Saudi Arabia	_____	riyal
Spain	_____	peseta

Country	Adjective	Currency
_____	Swedish	krona
Thailand	_____	baht
UK ⎰ England	_____	_____
UK ⎱ Britain	_____	
USA	_____	_____
USSR	_____	rouble
Venezuela	_____	bolivar

Note: If your country or others that you know are not included above, write them down together with their appropriate adjectives and currency.

Language use

Exercise 1
Plurality; fractions

A   The usual plural of *person* is *people* e.g. *one person*; *a lot of people*. *Population* is used to specify a number of people in a specific place e.g. a country.

B   With plural/countable nouns (e.g. *people*, *students*, *books*) it is usual to use *number* (as above).
With uncountable nouns (e.g. *information*, *advice*, *money*) it is usual to use *amount*. Compare the following:
    The *number* of students *is* increasing each year. ⎱ both use singular
    The *amount* of poverty *is* considerable.   ⎰ verb form

C   Notice the following constructions:

The	majority minority	of the	population people	live in poverty.
One-half 50 per cent				

There *were* 370 million people.
The number of people *was* 370 million.
The population *was* 370 million.

Each Every	person individual	is	poor.
All the	people population	are	

The *two* people are poor.
Both the people are poor.

1 Write one short paragraph describing the population of your country, making use of some of the language constructions shown above.

2 Fractions
  a Write in figures:
     one-half   one-sixth   one-third
  b Write in words:
     $\frac{1}{4}$ $\frac{2}{3}$ $\frac{3}{4}$
     $\frac{5}{6}$ $\frac{7}{8}$ $\frac{9}{10}$

Stage 2   Relative poverty and inequality

Comprehension

Pre-questions

Before you read the passage, read the following questions. Do you know the answers already? Discuss them with other students to see if they know the answers. The questions will help to give a purpose to your reading; it is not necessary to write the answers.

1 What is the basic difference between the size and functional distribution of income?
2 What changes would you expect in the size distribution of income in an LDC as *per capita* income grows?
3 Why is it that LDCs' governments will probably have difficulties in following fundamental aims of equality?

1   Many social scientists have argued that poverty cannot be discussed in isolation from the more general problem of inequality. Relative poverty or deprivation is defined with respect to what is considered to be 'normal' or 'socially acceptable' in any given society at any given time, and it thus brings
5   the distribution of income to the forefront of the discussion.[1]

The majority of LDCs are characterised by a variety of economic and social inequalities – inequalities in the distribution of income and wealth, between urban and rural areas, between different regions, tribes and ethnic groups and with respect to access to modern sector facilities (employment,
10   housing, education, health). Data are rarely available to illustrate the true dimensions of these various inequalities. Thus, alternative measures of the extent of inequality in the distribution of income are usually taken as indicators of the extent of inequality in general, given that economic and social inequalities interact with, and reinforce, one another.

15   Economists distinguish between the size distribution of income, which shows how many persons or families receive how much income, and the functional distribution of income, which divides income according to source (wages, profits, rent).

The World Bank (Chenery *et al.*, 1974, Ch. 1, Table 1.1, pp. 8 9) has
20   collected the available information on the size distribution of income for 66 developed and less developed countries, which shows markedly greater relative inequality in the latter than in the former. In the LDCs with the highest level of inequality, the richest 20 per cent of the population receive over 60 per cent of GNP, while the poorest 40 per cent of the population
25   receive 10 per cent or less. In addition, many would argue that the economic conditions of the poor appear to deteriorate, rather than improve, as a result of economic growth (Adelman and Morris, 1973).

Cross-country data on the size distribution of income have been utilised to investigate the relationship between economic growth and income
30   distribution over time. The available data tend to support the hypothesis, first advanced by Kuznets (1955), of an inverted U-shaped relationship between the level of economic development (as measured by *per capita*

income) and the degree of inequality (the empirical evidence is summarised
in Colman and Nixson, 1978, Ch. 3; Fields, 1980, Ch. 4).

35   Inequality is low in an unchanging, 'traditional' society, but rises as
economic growth accelerates. At some level of development the degree of
inequality reaches a maximum and subsequently declines as more 'mature'
levels of economic development are reached. Thus both very low and very
high levels of economic development are associated with greater income
40 equality.

Many economists have inferred from such data that there exists a trade-
off between economic growth and economic equality. If LDCs want to grow
rapidly, it is argued, they must be prepared to tolerate high and for a time
growing levels of inequality. It should be noted, however, that it is usually
45 the functional distribution of income (especially the division of income
between wages and profits) that such economists have in mind, on which
little reliable information exists. Others (for example, Myrdal, 1968) have
argued that greater economic and social equality are in fact necessary
preconditions for more rapid growth and development.

50   Despite the cross-country data, there are no theoretical and empirical
grounds for arguing that there is an inevitable conflict between equality and
growth, or that there exists a systematic pattern relating changes in
inequality to economic growth. Individual LDCs differ widely in these
matters and, as Fields (1980, p. 94) has argued:

55   'Growth itself does not determine a country's inequality course. Rather, the
       decisive factor is the type of economic growth as determined by the
       environment in which growth occurs and the political decisions taken.'

The distribution of income also has a functional value in the sense that
different distributional profiles will clearly have differing impacts on the
60 nature and characteristics of the process of economic growth and development in any given economy at any given time. The distribution of income
will be a partial determinant of savings and capital accumulation, patterns
of consumption, the composition of imports and through import-substituting industrialisation (see Unit 6), the composition and characteristics of the
65 output of the domestic manufacturing sector. Indirectly, it will influence the
choice of technology (see Unit 8), and the employment created (see Unit
5), within the 'modern' manufacturing sector.

Issues concerning the distribution of income are thus at the very centre of
the debate over what development *should* be (Unit 1) and how it can be
70 achieved. The latter point raises many difficult questions. How can the
governments of LDCs achieve the income distributions that they profess to
desire? Although in principle a variety of policy instruments exists to assist
the achievement of distributional objectives, in practice they are often
inadequate or ineffective. Privileged groups and classes will resist the
75 erosion of the economic, political and social benefits that they derive from
their position in society, and governments too, drawn from or dependent on
such classes or strata, are unlikely to pursue radical egalitarian objectives
even though they have been encouraged to do so by such institutions as the
World Bank (Chenery *et al.*, 1974) and the ILO (1972).

80   The most radical and far-reaching redistributions of income and wealth in recent years have occurred during, and as a part of, social and political upheavals of a fundamental kind. There are no compelling reasons for believing that this state of affairs will change in the immediate future.

[1] 'Poverty can be defined objectively and applied consistently only in terms of the concept of relative deprivation . . . Individuals, families and groups in the population can be said to be in poverty when they lack the resources to obtain the types of diets, participate in the activities and have the living conditions and amenities which are customary, or are widely encouraged or approved, in the societies to which they belong. Their resources are so seriously below those commanded by the average individual or family that they are, in effect, excluded from ordinary living patterns, customs and activities.' (Townsend, 1974, p. 15).

References

Adelman, I. and Morris, C. T. (1973), *Economic Growth and Social Equity in Developing Countries*, Stanford University Press.

Chenery, H. B. *et al.* (1974), *Redistribution With Growth*, Oxford University Press.

Colman, D. and Nixson, F. (1978), *Economics of Change in Less Developed Countries*, Oxford, Philip Allan.

Fields, G. S. (1980), *Poverty, Inequality, and Development*, Cambridge University Press.

International Labour Office (ILO), (1972), *Employment, Incomes and Equality: A Strategy for Increasing Productive Employment in Kenya*, Geneva.

Kuznets, S. (1955), 'Economic Growth and Income Inequality', *American Economic Review*, Vol. 45, No. 1, March.

Myrdal, G. (1968), *Asian Drama*, Harmondsworth, Penguin Books.

Srinivasan, T. N. (1977), 'Poverty: Some Measurement Problems', *World Bank Reprint Series*, No. 77

Townsend, P. (1974), 'Poverty as relative deprivation: resources and style of living' in D. Wedderburn (ed.), (1974), *Poverty, Inequality and Class Structure*, Cambridge University Press.

World Bank, *World Development Report 1980*, published for the World Bank by Oxford University Press.

Comprehension

Post-questions

After you have read the passage write brief answers to the following questions. Try to express your answers in your own words if possible.

1 Do indicators of inequality in the distribution of income perform any other function than indicating distribution of income inequality? If so, what?

2 In lines 28–40 reference is made to Kuznets and the inverted U-shaped relationship between the level of economic development and the degree of inequality. Read the two paragraphs carefully and then select from the four diagrams below the one that best represents the information given.

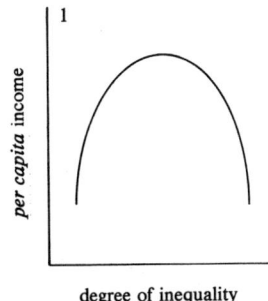

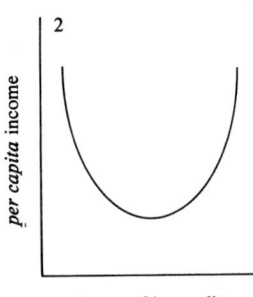

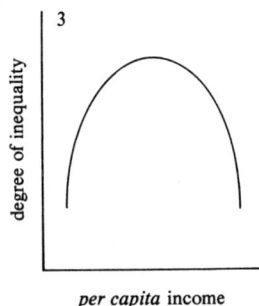

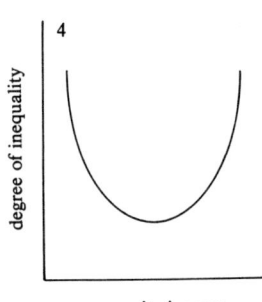

3 Is there any evidence to suggest that economic growth and economic (in)equality are related?

4 Give three examples of the areas that differing distributions of income can influence.

5 Are there any difficulties associated with how income redistribution can be achieved?

6 Does it seem likely that revolutions etc. will continue to be responsible for major redistributions of income and wealth?

Word study

Exercise 1
Alternative vocabulary

Below is a list of words (and line numbers) from the text (1–18). Next to them is a list of synonyms or explanations, in mixed order (a–r). Match the words from the text with their synonyms.

1 deprivation (3)	a	claim
2 urban (8)	b	sudden and violent change
3 markedly (21)	c	allow, permit, endure
4 deteriorate (26)	d	overwhelming, very strong
5 inverted (31)	e	lacking necessities or comforts
6 accelerate (36)	f	effect
7 inferred (41)	g	of a town or city
8 tolerate (43)	h	concluded
9 inevitable (51)	i	equalising
10 impact (59)	j	become worse, worsen
11 profess (71)	k	upside down
12 inadequate (74)	l	unavoidable
13 erosion (75)	m	become faster, increase
14 egalitarian (77)	n	disappearance, removal
15 far-reaching (80)	o	basic
16 upheaval (82)	p	insufficient
17 fundamental (82)	q	likely to have many consequences, having a wide influence or effect
18 compelling (82)	r	noticeably

Exercise 1B
Explanation

The following phrases are taken from the text (line numbers are given). Can you explain their meaning as used in the text? Use a dictionary if necessary.

1 in the latter than in the former (22)   3 a partial determinant (62)
2 a trade-off (41)

Language use

Exercise 1
Other, others, another

In this unit, and in others, there are several instances of the words *other*, *others*, *another* being used in different language constructions. Look carefully at the differences in use in the following examples (Unit and Stage numbers are given where appropriate).

A   Other
a There is an absence of unemployment benefits and *other* forms of social security. (5.2) *Note:* can be used before a plural noun

b *Other* data are not available. *Other* criteria must be specified.
Note: before a plural noun at the beginning of a sentence

c Is it preferable to obtain the technology through some *other* channel? (8.1) *Note:* used after words such as *some* and before a singular noun

d Perhaps in this area, more than in any *other*, there was general agreement. (3.2) *Note: other* stands for 'other area' – singular

e The neo-classical view of the world, *on the other hand*, is one of flexibility. (3.2). *Note:* a fixed expression comparing two items; often preceded by *on the one hand* . . .

B Others

f . . . make some patterns . . . more likely than *others*. (3.2)
Note: plural pronoun – stands for 'other patterns'

g *Others* have analysed the problem. (10.2)
Note: plural pronoun – stands for 'other people'

C Another

h This is one solution to the problem, but there is *another* difficulty.
Note: means '<u>one</u> other' – used with singular nouns only

i a The LDCs have at one time or *another* been colonies. (2.1)
  b . . . which in one way or *another* inhibits the expansion of output (10.2)
Note: **a** and **b** stand for 'another time' and 'another way' – singular

j Oligopolists compete with *one another*. (7.2)
Note: means 'each other' and can be used synonymously.

Use the appropriate words from the following list to complete the passage:
another, each other, one another, on the other hand, other, others

It is easy to say that a majority of people in LDCs live in absolute poverty. (1)_____ it is very difficult to define poverty, as it is a relative concept involving the distribution of income. Most LDCs are characterised by a variety of inequalities in the distribution of income and wealth. One such inequality is between urban and rural areas, while (2)_____ is between different regions. (3)_____ inequalities are between different tribes and ethnic groups. Yet (4)_____ concern access to facilities such as employment, housing, education and health.

Extension activities

1 Writing: A case study of poverty
Define poverty as it exists in your country. Describe a group of people that are known to be poor in your country: give some indication of their poverty and what you consider to be the causes of that poverty.

2 Group activity: Pyramid discussion
The procedure for conducting this activity is described on pages 7–8.
Select from the list below what you consider to be the three most important causes of poverty in LDCs. The order of the three choices is not important.

1 unemployment/disguised unemployment	16 low wages/income
2 early death of the main wage-earner	17 low productivity
3 large families/insufficient family planning	18 drink/gambling
4 illness/malnutrition/poor medical facilities	19 discrimination
5 bureaucratic corruption	20 inflexible religions
6 illiteracy/poor education	
7 high rents in rural areas	
8 inefficient government administration	
9 inequalities in the distribution of income and wealth	
10 limited access to land and other factors of production	
11 inadequately developed infrastructure	
12 lack of local credit facilities	
13 inefficient land utilisation	
14 poor climate and lack of natural resources	
15 insufficient investment for industrialisation	

Unit 5   Urbanisation and employment

Stage 1 Urbanisation in less developed countries (LDCs)

1 The level of urbanisation is usually measured by the percentage of the total population of a country living in urban areas. Between 1920 and 1970, the proportion of the world's population living in towns and cities increased from 19 to 37 per cent, and it is estimated that, by the year 2000, over one
5 half of the world's population is likely to be living in urban areas (World Bank, 1979, Ch. 6).

With respect to the LDCs, urban population grew at an average annual rate of 4 per cent between 1950 and 1980, and although some decline in the rate of growth is expected for the remainder of this century, nevertheless
10 the urban areas of the LDCs will still have to absorb an additional one billion people by the year 2000.

Given the high rate of urban population growth, the number of very large cities in the less developed world has expanded significantly. In 1950, only one city in the Third World had a population of over 5 million (Greater
15 Buenos Aires). By the year 2000, it is estimated that there will be 40 cities of or above this size, compared with only 12 in the industrialised countries. Eighteen cities in LDCs are expected to have populations of more than 10 million people, and Mexico City may well reach 30 million (World Bank, 1979, Ch. 6).
20 Urbanisation patterns differ markedly between different regions of the Third World, although the policy makers face similar problems in all areas. The major problems are concerned with the provision of urban employment opportunities, the provision of urban transport facilities and of adequate housing, health and educational facilities. Congestion and pollution are also
25 issues of increasing importance in a large number of urban areas in LDCs. On the more positive side, however, it should be noted that urbanisation also creates new opportunities for increases in productivity and incomes and the reduction of poverty.

In Stage 2, we look in greater detail at some of the issues relating to
30 employment and unemployment in the context of the urban areas of the LDCs.

Comprehension

A The following statements are based upon the information in the passage. If a statement is correct, write T (TRUE); if it is wrong, write F (FALSE).

1 The level of urbanisation is normally measured by the total population of a country living in towns and cities.

2 In the fifty years up to 1970 there was an 18 per cent increase in the proportion of the world's population living in urban areas.
3 An average annual rate of growth of 4 per cent in LDCs' urban population is expected to continue until the year 2000.
4 It is estimated that there will be 40 cities in the world with a population of 5 million or more by the year 2000.
5 There are big differences in the problems facing policy makers concerned with urbanisation in the LDCs.

B   Write brief answers to the following questions, obtaining your information from the passage.

1 What is the general trend in urbanisation throughout the world?
2 What are the predicted differences for the year 2000 between large cities in LDCs and those in developed countries?
3 What are the advantages and disadvantages of increased urbanisation in LDCs?

Word study

Exercise 1A
Alternative vocabulary

Below is a list of words (and line numbers) from the text (1–6). Next to them is a list of synonyms or explanations, in mixed order (a–f). Match the words from the text with their synonyms.

1 with respect to (7)	a take in
2 remainder (9)	b contamination
3 absorb (10)	c concerning, regarding
4 by (15)	d overcrowding
5 congestion (24)	e from now until, between now and
6 pollution (24)	f rest

Exercise 1B
Explanation

In line 11 the phrase 'one *billion* people' is used. Write down in figures what you understand by *a billion*. Then look at the Key.

Language use

Exercise 1
Prepositions with dates and figures

The following passage is based upon part of the Stage 1 text. Write down a suitable preposition for each numbered space. Do not look back at the Stage 1 text unless you have great difficulty.

(1)_____ 1920 and 1970, the proportion (2)_____ the world's population living (3)_____ towns and cities increased (4)_____ 19 per cent (5)_____ 37 per cent. Thus (6)_____ that period (7)_____ 50 years, world urbanisation increased (8)_____ 18 per cent. It is estimated that (9)_____ the year 2000, more than a half (10)_____ the world's population will probably be living (11)_____ urban areas. This means an increase (12)_____ (13)_____ least 14 per cent (14)_____ 30 years.
      (15)_____ LDCs, urban population grew (16)_____ an average annual rate (17)_____ 4 per cent (18)_____ the thirty years (19)_____ 1950 (20)_____ 1980. (21)_____ 1950, only one city (22)_____ the Third World had a population (23)_____ over 5 million. (24)_____ the year 2000 it is estimated that there will be 40 cities (25)_____ or above this size, compared (26)_____ only 12 (27)_____ the industrial countries.

**Exercise 2
Information transfer –
a graph**

The following outline graph can be used to show some of the information contained in the first part of the text. Compose a suitable title for the graph. Label the vertical and horizontal axes. From the information at the beginning of the text, plot some positions on the graph (by means of a small 'x') and then draw straight lines to link the positions.

Figure 5.1

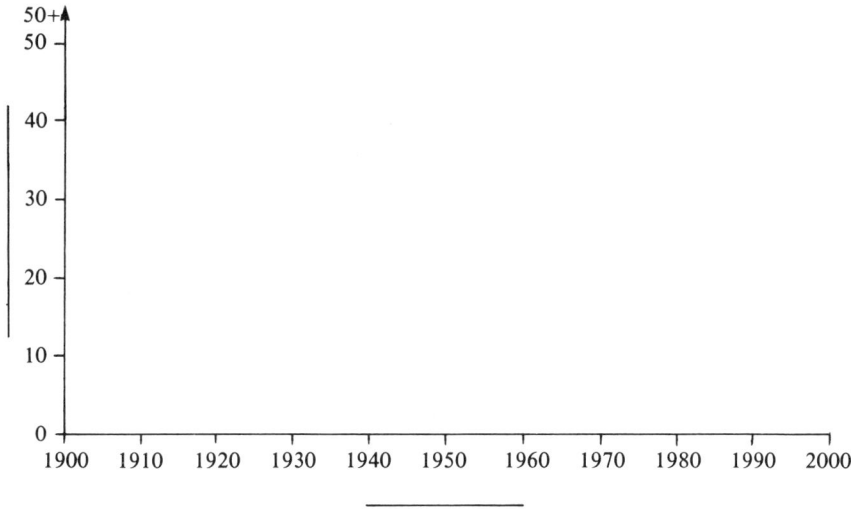

Stage 2 Employment and unemployment in the urban context

Comprehension

Pre-questions

Before you read the passage, read the following questions. Do you know the answers already? Discuss them with other students to see if they know the answers. The questions will help to give a purpose to your reading; it is not necessary to write the answers.

1 Is there any difference in meaning in the term 'unemployed' as used in developed countries and as used in LDCs?
2 Why has more emphasis now been put on the urban informal sector?
3 Give some examples of urban informal sector activities. What are the advantages of such activities?

---

1   The question of employment and unemployment in LDCs has been raised in a number of previous units. In Unit 1, Stage 2, it was noted that the reduction in unemployment is a commonly accepted objective of economic development. In Unit 4, Stage 2, we referred to the interaction between
5   inequality and employment. Many (for example, the International Labour Office – ILO) would argue that the creation of employment opportunities is an important step towards reducing inequalities in the distribution of income. In Unit 3, Stage 1, the concepts of 'employment' and 'unemployment' in the context of LDCs were given as examples of 'misplaced
10   aggregation'.

A deep concern with problems relating to employment, unemployment, underemployment, 'disguised' unemployment and surplus labour has always been central to the discussion of economic development. The very concept of development itself presupposes the fuller mobilisation and
15 utilisation of the great reserves of (mainly) unskilled labour that are to be found in most LDCs. The ILO has estimated that, in 1977, out of 767 million workers in LDCs (excluding China and other centrally planned economies) some 40 million were unemployed and a further 291 million underemployed, totalling 331 million in all and representing 43 per cent of
20 the labour force (Plant, 1983, p. 11).

The discussion of these issues has, however, generated much controversy. The concept of 'employment' presupposes a 'fairly homogeneous, mobile labour force, willing and able to work and responsive to incentives' (Streeten, 1972, p. 55). Such conditions do not always exist in LDCs, and
25 thus the notion of a 'labour force' must be treated with great care. In addition, in a society where unemployment benefits or social security payments are not available, to be unemployed in the sense that that term is used in a developed capitalist economy would imply that one would eventually starve to death, unless one could live off friends or relatives
30 (possible in the short run, but not in the longer run).

The concept of 'unemployment' has thus been largely replaced with the concepts of 'disguised' or 'under' employment. People in LDCs may work very hard for long hours, but produce very little (they are said to have a low or zero marginal productivity) and hence receive low incomes. Their lack of
35 access to land, capital and other productive factors and education and health facilities, coupled with social and cultural attitudes and institutional structures, are together responsible for their low productivity and continued poverty.

Attention was originally focused on the definition and measurement of
40 underemployment in the rural sector of the economy. More recently, however, attention has shifted to the problems arising from substantial rural–urban migration and the subsequent rapid urban population growth (Stage 1), together with the failure of the 'modern' sector of the urban economy to generate sufficient new job opportunities both to absorb the
45 existing pool of unemployed persons and to provide work for new entrants to the labour force.

This shift in emphasis was associated with what Moser (1978) has identified as a move from the preoccupation with unemployment 'to the identification of *employment* as the most important problem in the
50 developing countries'. She continues:

'It was the recognition that low levels of unemployment exist where there is an absence of unemployment benefits and other forms of social security, forcing the adult population to find some means of livelihood, legal or illegal, which resulted in the identification of the "working poor" as the target group
55 requiring specific attention. The fact that a majority in this group tend to find work or remuneration in small-scale enterprises and activities within the so-called "informal sector" of the economy led to an emphasis on this sector.'

(Moser, 1978, p. 1051)

The urban informal sector is defined so as to contrast it with the modern,
60 formal sector of the urban economy. Although definitions and conceptual-
isations differ, most authorities on the urban informal sector would agree
that it largely consists of economic activities with a number of distinct
characteristics: ease of entry into the activity concerned, reliance on local
resources, labour-intensive, small-scale operations, family ownership, skills
65 obtained outside the formal educational system and unregulated and
competitive markets. Examples of such activities include petty trading,
small repair workshops, the recycling of waste materials (for example,
making sandals from automobile tyres), beer brewing and so on.

The World Employment Programme of the ILO has focused attention on
70 the labour-intensity of the techniques used in this sector, the 'appropriate-
ness' of its products (see Unit 8, Stage 2) and its flexibility and dynamism.
The ILO recommends that governments in LDCs should encourage, rather
than restrict, the development of informal sector activities in order to
encourage the creation of more employment opportunities at the lowest
75 possible cost.

The problem of employment in LDCs is, however, a complex and multi-
dimensional one. Its causes are varied and there are no easy answers to the
problems that it poses for the governments of LDCs. Obviously, more jobs,
in both urban and rural areas, will have to be created, but more
80 fundamental issues relating to the strategies of development selected, and
the objectives of development pursued, will have to be confronted before
effective, longer-run solutions begin to be identified and implemented.

References

Moser, Caroline O. N. (1978), 'Informal Sector or Petty Commodity Production: Dualism or Dependence in Urban Development?' *World Development*, Vol. 6, No. 9/10, pp. 1041–1064.

Plant, R. (1983), *A Short Guide to the ILO World Employment Programme*, ILO, Geneva.

Streeten, P. (1972), *The Frontiers of Development Studies*, London, Macmillan.

World Bank (1979), *World Development Report 1979*, Washington DC, World Bank.

Comprehension

Post-questions

After you have read the passage write brief answers to the following questions. Try to express your answers in your own words if possible.

1 Why is it necessary to be careful when considering the concept of a 'labour force' in LDCs?
2 What causes the low productivity of workers in LDCs?
3 Why has it been suggested that *employment* is the most important problem in LDCs?
4 What are the main characteristics of the urban informal sector activities?
5 Is the creation of more jobs the sole (or the most important) task facing LDCs' governments?

Word study

Exercise 1A
Alternative vocabulary

Below is a list of words (and line numbers) from the text (1–19). Next to them is a list of synonyms or explanations, in mixed order (a–s). Match the words from the text with their synonyms.

1 presupposes (14)	a creates
2 homogeneous (22)	b stock or reservoir
3 incentives (23)	c notions
4 term (27)	d faced
5 live off (29)	e assumes, takes for granted
6 lack (34)	f small-scale, minor
7 coupled (36)	g obtain money from, depend or rely on
8 shifted (41)	h light open shoes with straps
9 pool (45)	i expression
10 livelihood (53)	j payment, reward
11 target (54)	k similar, uniform
12 remuneration (56)	l employment, earning a wage (living)
13 conceptualisations (60)	m moved, transferred
14 reliance (63)	n combined, joined
15 petty (66)	o carried out, put into effect
16 sandals (68)	p dependence
17 poses (78)	q encouragement, motivation
18 confronted (81)	r want, need, deficiency
19 implemented (82)	s objective, mostly affected

Exercise 1B
Explanation

The following words are taken from the text (line numbers are given). Can you explain their meaning as used in the text? Use a dictionary if necessary.

1 disguised unemployment (12)
2 recycling (67)

Exercise 2
Employ/employment

From the verb *to employ* a lot of words are formed that are frequently used in economics. Look carefully at the diagram below to see the relationships between the words.

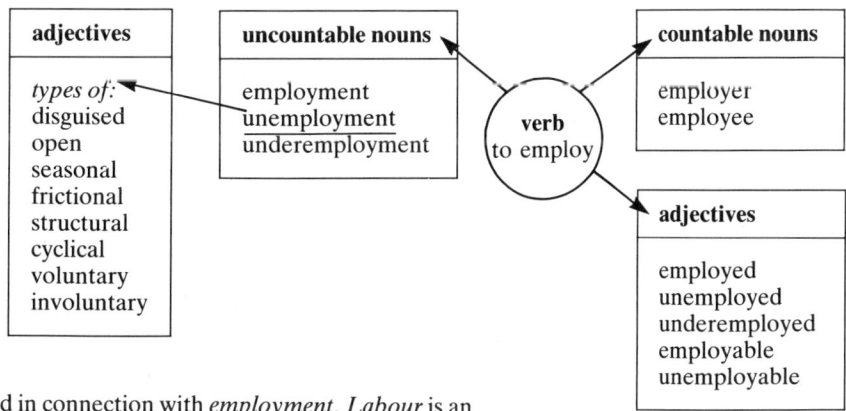

Note: Related vocabulary:
To work and *labour* are often used in connection with *employment*. *Labour* is an uncountable noun meaning 'workers' (considered as a class).
employee = worker
labourer = unskilled manual worker
work-force = labour-force (i.e. the total number of workers engaged or available)
to labour = to work hard

Open exercise

Show that you understand the meanings of the words given below, and that you can use them correctly, by composing sentences that in some way explain their meaning (perhaps by giving a definition).

e.g. An *employee* is a person who works for someone else in return for payment.

1 full employment	3 unemployed	5 employer
2 seasonal unemployment	4 work-force	6 labourer

Language use

Exercise 1
Although and but

In this book there are many examples of *although* and *but* being used with similar meaning. *Although* means 'in spite of the fact that'.
Look carefully at the following examples. They show two sentences joined together by *although* or *but*:

They worked very hard. They produced very little.

1 *Although* they worked very hard, they produced very little.
2 They worked very hard, *but* they produced very little.
3 They produced very little, *(al)though* they worked very hard.

Note: Constructions 1 and 2 are frequently used to mean the same thing. Construction 3 can also be used but it changes the emphasis.
A common mistake is to use *Although* at the beginning of a sentence together with *but* in the same sentence. One or the other should be used, not both.

The following sentences are taken from the first five units in the book. Join the first three pairs together using *Although* at the beginning. Join the last three pairs together using *but* in the sentence.

Although

1a Frank's ideas have been extremely influential.
  b They have been increasingly criticised.

2a Seers conceded that certain elementary propositions retained their general validity in the context of LDCs.
  b He was particularly critical of the application of macro-economic concepts and models.

3a Inequality is low in a traditional society.
  b It rises as economic growth accelerates.

But

4a Seers, Streeten and other like-minded economists mounted a powerful and sustained onslaught on orthodox economics.
  b The established orthodoxy was by no means defeated.

5a In principle a variety of policy instruments exists to assist the achievement of distributional objectives.
  b In practice they are often inadequate or ineffective.

6a Some decline in the rate of growth of urban population is expected for the remainder of this century.
  b The urban areas of the LDCs will still have to absorb an additional one billion people by the year 2000.

**Exercise 2
Information transfer –
a pie chart/diagram**

The following pie chart can be used to show the information contained in the second paragraph of the text. Compose a suitable title for it. Two of the segments contain some information: complete the information and also complete the third segment.

Figure 5.2 _____

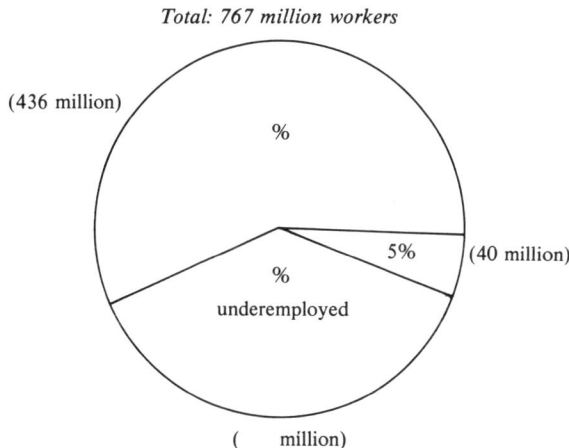

Total: 767 million workers

(436 million)

%

(40 million)
5%

%
underemployed

(million)

Extension activities

1 Writing: Essay

Describe the employment situation in your country. Where appropriate refer to different types of unemployment (see Exercise 2 Employment) and any other aspects of employment mentioned in the text.

2 Group activity: Discussion – role-play

Minimum wages
Imagine that you are the minister, in the government of an LDC, responsible for fixing minimum wage levels in all sectors of the economy. Look at the list of 12 occupations in the table below. Decide on the order of the 12 occupations: write the highest wage first (1) and the lowest last (12). (Actual wages in monetary terms are not required, just the order.) Note that several jobs can be at the same level if you wish.

Individually decide on the order of the occupations and then discuss your order with others in a group. Be prepared to justify the order you have chosen (and think of the effects on the economy). Bear in mind some of the following, possible, criteria for determining wage levels: production *v.* service, scarce *v.* plentiful supply, skilled *v.* unskilled, working conditions, demand, differentials, limited resources, social desirability . . .

nurse	secondary school teacher
farm labourer	policeman/woman
bank clerk (cashier)	shop assistant
road builder (labourer)	civil servant
university lecturer	factory worker (semi-skilled)
civil engineer	medical doctor

Unit 6   The industrialisation of less developed countries (LDCs)

Stage 1 Statistical overview

1 For the majority of LDCs, industrialisation remains a fundamental objective of economic development. Only through industrialisation, it is argued, can the LDCs achieve and sustain rapid rates of economic growth, create more employment opportunities, diversify and modernise their economies
5 and provide for the basic needs of their populations. In global terms, it is the longer-term objective of the LDCs that, by the year 2000, they should account for at least 25 per cent of world manufacturing value added, as compared to an estimated 10.3 per cent in 1981 (all data taken from UNIDO, 1982).

10 Between 1960 and 1970, manufacturing value added in the LDCs grew on average by 7.3 per cent *per annum* (at constant prices). The corresponding figure for the period 1970–81 was 5.8 per cent *per annum*. Classifying LDCs according to income groups, however, highlights the fact that the slowing down in the rate of growth was most pronounced for those LDCs with the
15 lowest (less than US \$265 *per capita* in 1965) and the highest (over US \$2,000 *per capita*) incomes. For the so-called 'upper-middle income' countries (US \$1,075–2,000 *per capita*) there was a slight acceleration in the growth of manufacturing value added to 8.5 per cent *per annum* (1970–1978) as compared to 7.7 per cent *per annum* in the earlier period.

20 The figures above indicate increasing differentiation between different LDCs and, combined with marked regional variations in shares and rates of growth of manufacturing value added, clearly illustrate the uneven spread of economic growth and industrialisation in the less developed world (see also Unit 1). Indeed, rapid and sustained industrialisation has been
25 confined to relatively few countries, and UNIDO (1979, Table 11.6, p. 42) has calculated that for the period 1966–75, ten LDCs (Brazil, Mexico, Argentina, Republic of Korea, India, Turkey, Iran, Indonesia, Hong Kong and Thailand) were responsible for almost 75 per cent of the *increase* in manufacturing value added for all LDCs. Many LDCs, therefore, especially
30 the so-called least developed (mainly concentrated in sub-Saharan Africa) have yet to experience significant industrial development and the structural change associated with it.

Comprehension

A The following statements are based upon the information in the passage. If a statement is correct, write T (TRUE); if it is wrong, write F (FALSE).

1 It is argued that LDCs can only change and update their economies through industrialisation.

2 In the long run the worldwide aim of LDCs is to account for only a quarter of world manufacturing value added.

3 Between 1970 and 1981 the slowing down in the rate of growth was most noticeable for LDCs with less than US $265 and with over US $2,000 *per capita* income.

4 The figures of growth quoted show that there are fewer and fewer differences between LDCs.

5 Ten LDCs have not yet experienced any important industrial development.

B   Write brief answers to the following questions, obtaining your information from the passage.

1 Is it the long-term aim of LDCs to account for 10.3 per cent of world manufacturing value added? If not, what is the aim?

2 If LDCs are classified according to income groups, what pattern emerges regarding rates of economic growth?

3 Which income group of LDCs grew the fastest between 1960 and 1970, and what was their growth rate?

4 How would you describe the process of industrialisation among LDCs?

Word study

Exercise 1A
Alternative vocabulary

Below is a list of words (and line numbers) from the text (1–6). Next to them is a list of synonyms or explanations, in mixed order (a–f). Match the words from the text with their synonyms.

1	diversify (4)	a	unequal, irregular
2	global (5)	b	as named by others
3	pronounced (14)	c	kept, restricted, limited
4	so-called (16)	d	vary production
5	uneven (22)	e	strongly marked
6	confined (25)	f	worldwide

Exercise 1B
Explanation

In line 11 the term *constant prices* is used. Can you explain its meaning as used in the text? Use a dictionary if necessary.

Exercise 2
Industry, industrialise, manufacture

In this unit language associated with *industrialisation* is used. Look carefully at the following frequently used words.

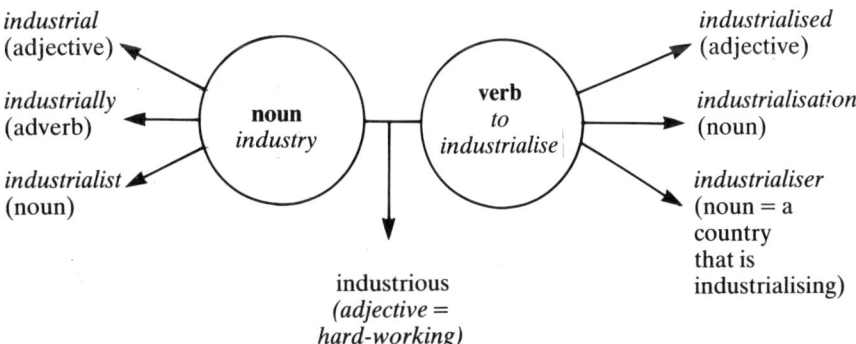

industrial (adjective)
industrially (adverb)
industrialist (noun)
noun *industry*
verb *to industrialise*
industrialised (adjective)
industrialisation (noun)
industrialiser (noun = a country that is industrialising)
industrious (adjective = hard-working)

(Note: The verb and the words on the right can be written with z instead of s e.g. *industrialized)*

Pronunciation note: in<u>dus</u>try has the main stress on the first syllable. All the other words have the main stress on the second syllable e.g. *in<u>dus</u>trialise*.

In conjunction with *industry* the verb *to manufacture* is frequently used. Nouns are *manufacture*, *manufactures* and *manufacturer*. Phrases commonly used are: *manufacturing value added . . . manufactured goods . . .*

Use the appropriate words from those shown above (or formed from those shown above) to complete the following sentences.

1 A(n) (1)_____ is a person who has a big interest in the ownership or control of an (2)_____ enterprise, especially a factory owner.

2 A(n) (3)_____ is a person or firm responsible for (4)_____ goods.

3 After the Second World War many economists considered that (5)_____ was the best way for developing countries to develop. Thus priority was given to the development of (6)_____ .

4 From 1750 to 1830 the (7)_____ Revolution took place in Britain. It was based upon the textile (8)_____ and, in particular, the (9)_____ of cotton cloth. This Revolution transformed Britain into an (10)_____ nation.

Language use

Exercise 1
Information transfer –
a histogram or bar chart

The following bar chart can be used to show some of the information contained in the second paragraph of the text. Compose a suitable title for it. Label the vertical axis and the horizontal axis. In addition, label as many parts of the bar chart as you can (some parts have been done for you).

Figure 6.1

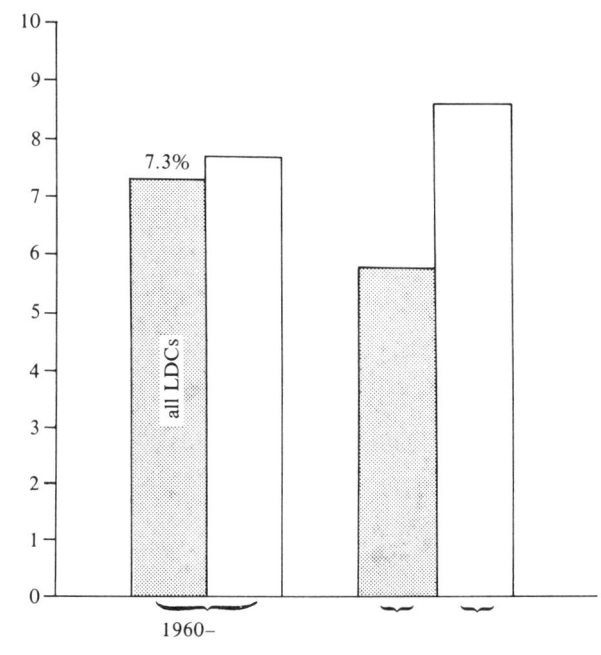

Stage 2 Industrialisation: strategies and performance

Comprehension

Pre-questions

Before you read the passage, read the following questions. Do you know the answers already? Discuss them with other students to see if they know the answers. The questions will help to give a purpose to your reading; it is not necessary to write the answers.

1 What is the main difference between import-substituting industrialisation (ISI) and export-led industrialisation?
2 What are some of the criticisms that have been made of ISI policies?
3 How important are manufactured goods in LDC exports?

1 A broad distinction may be drawn between strategies of industrialisation based predominantly on the production for the domestic market of manufactured goods previously imported (import-substituting industrialisation – ISI), and strategies based on the production of manufactured goods
5 for overseas markets (export-led industrialisation).

These are not mutually exclusive strategies, and elements of both may well be present in specific industrialisation efforts. In addition, individual industries and industrial activities have varying characteristics, and alternative classificatory systems can be adopted – for example, large-scale versus
10 small-scale, capital-intensive versus labour-intensive, urban-based versus rural-based, a dependence on local capital versus foreign capital.

In practice, the individual industry-mix and its associated characteristics tend to be determined by the overall strategy adopted. For example, the strategy of ISI, widely adopted by the majority of LDCs in the post-Second
15 World War period, typically involves the establishment of large-scale, capital-intensive, urban-based industries, catering largely to the needs of middle- and upper-income groups (see Unit 4). These are not the inevitable characteristics of ISI *per se*, but rather the outcome of a strategy of industrialisation which takes as given existing economic, political and
20 institutional structures and the extensive penetration of the economy by foreign capital and technology (both process and product – see Unit 8).

Many economists, especially those of the neo-classical school (see Unit 3) now argue that ISI has failed both as an industrialisation and as a development strategy. Excessively high tariff barriers and other protective
25 devices have encouraged the overdevelopment of import-substituting industries, and the absence of foreign competition has permitted the development of high-cost, inefficient, monopolistic and over-diversified industrial sectors. Widespread government intervention in these economies, it is alleged, has led to distortions in both product and factor markets,
30 turning the domestic terms of trade against the agricultural sector and encouraging the use of capital-intensive technologies (see Unit 8). Overvalued exchange rates have discriminated against exports and, combined

with the generally 'inward-looking' nature of ISI, have contributed to the continued balance of payments problems of the LDCs (see Unit 9).

35   Structuralists and dependency theorists are also critical of the consequences of the strategy of ISI. They argue that industrialisation, once seen as the solution to the problems of underdevelopment and poverty, has now become part of the problem itself. ISI has created, *inter alia*, a 'dependent' industrial structure, dominated by foreign capital and technology and
40   lacking a capital goods (that is, a machine-making) sector.

The neo-classical critique of ISI has produced an influential set of policy prescriptions. Trade restrictions should be lowered and rationalised, the exchange rate devalued and greater freedom should be given to the market, allowing it to generate the 'correct' price signals which will ensure a more
45   efficient allocation of resources. It is argued that domestic industries should be promoted, rather than protected. That is, the government should implement policies which eliminate or offset the disadvantages from which domestic industries suffer, through, for example, training programmes aimed at alleviating the shortage of skilled labour in the LDC. In general,
50   government policies should be such as to provide equal incentives for production for both the domestic and foreign market.

The experience of the export-led industrialisers appears to provide strong support for the neo-classical case. Between 1960 and 1977, the average real growth rate of manufactured exports from LDCs was 12.3 per cent *per*
55   *annum*, over twice that of their total merchandise exports (World Bank, 1980, Table 3 A.4). As a result of this trend, there has been a significant change in the composition of LDC exports, with the share of manufactured goods in total merchandise exports (excluding mineral fuels and related products) rising from 25.4 per cent in 1965 to 45.1 per cent in 1976
60   (UNIDO, 1979, Table V.1).

The four economies that are generally regarded as the most successful examples of export-led industrialisation – Hong Kong, Singapore, Republic of Korea and Taiwan – together accounted for over 60 per cent of all LDC manufactured goods exports in 1976. A number of other countries (Brazil,
65   Mexico, Argentina, Malaysia) have also increasingly adopted 'outward-oriented' strategies and have raised their share of LDC manufactured exports over this period, whereas the share of the more 'traditional' exporters, such as India and Pakistan, has dropped significantly (although in absolute terms these two economies remain important exporters of
70   manufactured goods).

An important change has also occurred in the composition of manufactured goods exports from the Newly Industrialising Countries (NICs – as the successful export-led industrialisers and the 'post-ISI' or 'transitional' economies such as Brazil and Mexico are sometimes referred to). The share
75   of finished products (for example, clothing) and more technically sophisticated goods (for example, machinery and transport equipment, electronic goods, etc.) has increased dramatically and, *ceterus paribus*, this is a trend that is likely to continue.

The NICs are held up as models of development that other LDCs should
80 follow. They have undoubtedly experienced high rates of growth of output
and employment, but the export-led strategy of industrialisation is not
without problems. Their continued export growth is highly dependent on
the economic performance of the advanced capitalist economies which
absorb approximately two-thirds of their manufactured exports (World
85 Bank, 1980, Table 3.3) and they are highly vulnerable to the increasingly
widespread 'new protectionism' in those economies ('orderly' marketing
arrangements, 'voluntary' export restraints, support for domestic industries
faced with high import penetration, etc.).

In addition, export-led industrialisation does not automatically solve the
90 balance of payments problem (domestic industries are import-intensive;
exports are heavily subsidised), nor does it eliminate poverty and unemployment (the costs of labour must be kept low in order to maintain the
competitive advantage). It may well induce a dependence on foreign capital
and technology very similar to that exhibited by the ISI 'model'.

95 The 'structuralist' policy prescriptions which follow from their critique of
ISI include, as a minimum, the regulation of TNCs, the development of a
domestic capital goods sector and the encouragement of indigenous
technological development, and the creation of mass markets for the output
of domestic industries, via income and asset redistribution (for example,
100 land reform) and increased government expenditure.

In an ideal world, some combination of neo-classical and structuralist
policies would perhaps make the most sense, but that would presuppose a
degree of political harmony and commitment to shared objectives that is
not likely to be found in many LDCs at the present time.

References

United Nations Industrial Development Organisation (UNIDO) (1979), *World Industry Since 1960: Progress and Prospects*,
New York.

UNIDO (1982), *A Statistical Review of the
World Industrial Situation 1981*, Vienna.
World Bank (1980), *World Development
Report 1980*, Oxford University Press.

Comprehension

Post-questions

After you have read the passage write brief answers to the following
questions. Try to express your answers in your own words if possible.

1 What are the typical characteristics of import-substituting
industrialisation as demonstrated by many LDCs after 1945?
2 What do the critics of ISI who are structuralists and dependency
theorists consider have been the consequences of ISI policies?
3 How important have manufactured goods been in exports from LDCs
after 1960?
4 Has the export-led strategy of industrialisation been completely successful in the Newly Industrialising Countries (NICs)? If not, explain why.
5 What is the 'structuralist' approach to some of the problems created by
ISI?

c

Word study

Exercise 1A
Alternative vocabulary

Below is a list of words (and line numbers) from the text (1–20). Next to them is a list of synonyms or explanations, in mixed order (a–t). Match the words from the text with their synonyms.

1 broad (1)	a declared, claimed
2 predominantly (2)	b compensate for, balance
3 mutually exclusive (6)	c mostly, mainly
4 overall (13)	d taken over, chosen and followed
5 catering to (16)	e shown, demonstrated
6 takes as given (19)	f separate and unable to exist together
7 penetration (20)	g discouraged
8 permitted (26)	h total
9 over-diversified (27)	i cause, bring about
10 widespread (28)	j general
11 alleged (29)	k complex
12 discriminated against (32)	l making provision for, supplying what is required
13 rationalised (42)	m goods
14 offset (47)	n influencing, controlling
15 alleviating (49)	o reducing
16 merchandise (55)	p extending over a large area
17 adopted (65)	q reorganised efficiently
18 sophisticated (75)	r takes for granted, assumes
19 induce (93)	s too varied
20 exhibited (94)	t allowed, made possible

Exercise 1B
Explanation

The following words are taken from the text (line numbers are given). Can you explain their meaning as used in the text? Use a dictionary if necessary.

1 tariff barriers (24)   **3** terms of trade (30)
2 monopolistic (27)   **4** balance of payments (34)

Language use

Exercise 1
Cause and effect

In economics writing, cause and effect occur quite frequently, even though these two words themselves may not be used. *Cause* may be equivalent to *reason* or *purpose*, and *effect* may be synonymous with *consequence*, *result* or *solution*. The relationship between the two may be expressed in a number of ways. Some examples are shown below.

cause (or reason)	**connective**	**effect** (or consequence etc.)
Demand has increased.	Therefore, As a result, As a consequence, Consequently, Because of this, Thus, For this reason, Accordingly, So,	prices will rise.

Similarly:

An increase in demand often	causes results in leads to produces	higher an increase in } prices.

Note: The 'effect' may come before the 'cause', as below:

effect	**connective**		**cause**
Prices will rise	because of as a result of on account of owing to through		an increase in demand.
	because since as	there is	
	because the demand has increased.		

In the Stage 2 text there are a number of examples of the cause/effect relationship:

'Excessively high tariff barriers and other protective devices . . . the overdevelopment of import-substituting industries.'

For the symbol '. . .', the words *have encouraged* are used in the text, but we could also use the following words: *have caused* or *have resulted in* or *have led to* or *have produced* etc.

1 Some sentences have been taken from the text and slightly shortened. They are separated into the parts of 'cause' and 'effect'. Find the sentences in the text and write down the appropriate verb or phrase (connective) that links them.

a The absence of foreign competition _____ the development of high-cost, inefficient, monopolistic and over-diversified industrial sectors. (26)

b Widespread government intervention in these economies _____ distortions in both product and factor markets. (28)

c Overvalued exchange rates _____ the continued balance of payments problems of the LDCs. (31)

d Export-led industrialisation _____ a dependence on foreign capital and technology. (84)

Now look carefully at the following sentence: it is organised differently from the sentences above. Find the connective, and say which part is the 'cause' and which part is the 'effect'.

e As a result of this trend, there has been a significant change in the composition of LDC exports.

2 **Open exercise**   Complete the following sentences by first adding an appropriate connective and then the remainder of the sentence.

a A rapid increase in urban population . . .

b Increased employment opportunities in LDCs . . .

c Low incomes . . .

Exercise 2
Should: prescription

In the text there are a number of examples of *should* being used as a prescription ('to prescribe'). This form is often used to give advice and is used as an alternative to *ought to*. Look carefully at the following examples:

neo-classical policy prescriptions (from line 41 onwards)

A   passive verbs

trade restrictions		lowered and rationalised . . .
the exchange rate	should be	devalued . . .
greater freedom		given to the market . . .
domestic industries		promoted . . .

B   active verbs

the government		implement policies . . .
government policies	should	provide equal incentives . . .
other LDCs		follow the NICs . . .

Now look at lines 95–100 in which you will find *structuralist policy prescriptions* listed. Write them out in a similar way to those shown above.

Extension activities

1 Writing: Essay

Select either your own country or one whose economy you have some knowledge of. Describe any attempts that have been made to industrialise the economy and discuss the effects of those attempts. What, in your opinion, should be prescribed in order to assist the industrialisation process?

2 Group activity: Role-play – discussion

Industrialisation of a developing country
Below is outlined a general economic development problem, but with sufficient information to make it possible to discuss it in some detail and to arrive at some general conclusions.

If possible, it should be discussed by groups of three (or four). If there are three to a group, each student takes the role of one of the ministers outlined below, with specific information for that combined ministry. The Minister for Finance and Foreign Affairs should be the Prime Minister (or Chairman, for the discussion). If there are four students, the fourth one should act as Prime Minister and make notes of the main conclusions reached.

The group should discuss the problem within a time limit (perhaps 30 minutes), make notes of the main conclusions, and give these in the form of an oral report to other students who have been simultaneously discussing the same problem. Each group can give its report, with questions from other groups and discussion to follow.

Problem: The government of a developing country (an imaginary one) – known as ASA – is trying to obtain £100 million to invest in industries in order to develop the country. *Consider:* how it can *obtain* the money, and how it can *invest* it in order to achieve the maximum effect in the short run but bearing in mind the long-term effects.

During the discussion consider, among other things, the following:
1 the level of employment
2 the type of education to be developed
3 the system of transport
4 the efficiency of agriculture
5 the availability of natural resources
6 the possibility of expanding existing industries or creating others
7 the role of taxation in the country
8 the role of the banks
9 the balance of payments position

The three ministers are as follows:
A   Minister for Employment, Education and Communications
B   Minister for Agriculture, Natural Resources and Industry
C   Minister for Finance and Foreign Affairs

Each minister has certain information to help him or her make some decisions: s/he should consider this carefully. It is given under the map of ASA below. Important items of information are underlined.

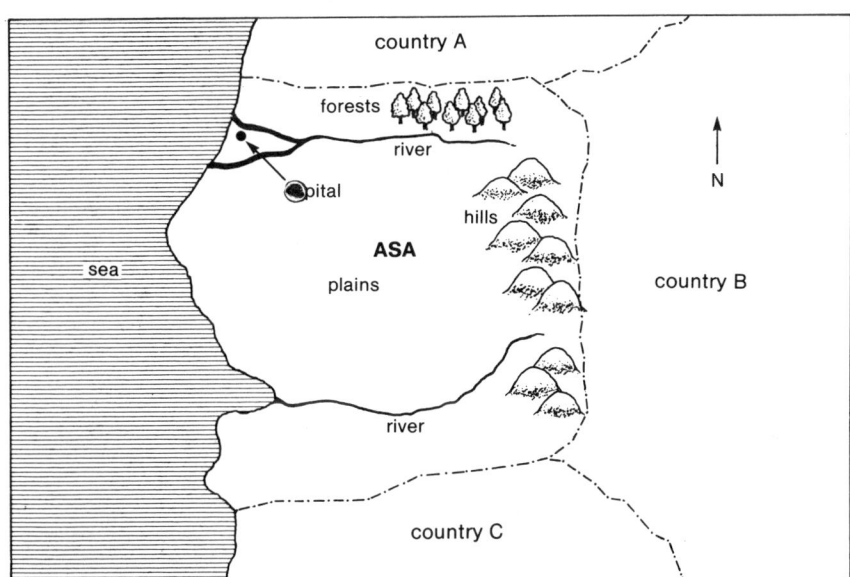

A   *Minister for Employment, Education and Communications*

1   The population of ASA is 20 million of whom 7 million are the working population (labour force). The population growth rate is 3 per cent p.a. 70 per cent of the working population is engaged in agriculture. 20 per cent of the labour force is unemployed at the moment.

2   There is nearly universal primary education. There is some secondary education, largely for the 'middle-classes', but this is slowly expanding to include other groups. There is one university of the traditional type. The university students are on strike at the moment (because they are dissatisfied with their job prospects when they leave university). There is a 40 per cent illiteracy rate in the country.

3   There are no railways. There are a number of large navigable rivers. A reasonable road network is under construction; it might be completed in about two years' time.

B   *Minister for Agriculture, Natural Resources and Industry*

1   The staple crop is grain (i.e. rice, wheat etc.), grown on the large plains in the west of the country. The country is normally self-sufficient in grain and often exports some to neighbouring countries. Last year the crops failed because of drought. There are some dairy cattle but not on a large scale. The farms are organised in small units.

2   There are reasonable quantities of natural resources in the form of copper and coal located in the foothills to the east of the country: these have not been mined to any great extent. There is a plentiful supply of timber in the forests in the north-east of the country. Diamonds have just been discovered in the extreme east of the country.

3   Most of the industry is small-scale cottage industries largely producing handicrafts. Some small-scale domestic consumption goods industries have just been started.

C   *Minister for Finance and Foreign Affairs* (and Prime Minister)

1   Very little revenue is raised by income tax; the *per capita* income at present is £200 p.a. Other forms of taxation are being considered. There are some import duties levied on imported consumer goods.

2   The banking system is not well developed. Banks exist only in the capital city and two other large towns. The banks are managed by Europeans and Americans.

3   Last year ASA imported more than it exported: there was, therefore, a deficit in the balance of payments of about £5 million which was covered by borrowing and the running down of the country's international reserves. Recently, ASA applied for a loan from the World Bank but it is not very hopeful of obtaining it (or it believes it will only get a small one).

Unit 7   The transnational corporation

Stage 1   Definition

1   The most straightforward definition of a transnational corporation (TNC)[1] is that it is an enterprise which controls assets – factories, mines, sales offices and the like – in two or more countries. On this definition, the United Nations estimated that in 1977 there were 10,373 firms with at least
5   one foreign affiliate. If we specify other criteria, e.g. the possession of a minimum number of affiliates or operation in a minimum number of host countries, the TNC population will be reduced. In 1977, there were 5,586 firms which operated in two or more host countries and there were 2,050 firms which operated in six or more host countries. The use of these
10   additional criteria affects the distribution by origin of TNCs. For example, TNCs from the United States of America account for 26.8 per cent of all firms with one or more foreign affiliates which operate in one or more host countries but for 36.9 per cent of all firms which operate in six or more host countries. These data partially illustrate the dominance, by virtue of their
15   size, of US TNCs – the share of US TNCs in the total TNC population rises as the minimum size of the corporation increases. Various measures of foreign content (exports, sales, assets, earnings or employment) can also be used in defining TNCs as can criteria relating to organisational form, motivation and the structure of decision-making or control in the TNC. It is
20   clear, therefore, that there are many possible ways of defining TNCs, and the United Nations has argued that '. . . undue stress need not be laid on the determination of a single, all-purpose definition of transnational corporations . . . various working definitions can be utilised for specific purposes' (UN, 1979, p. 7).

[1] also known as a multinational corporation (MNC)

Comprehension   A   The following statements are based upon the information in the passage. If a statement is correct, write T (TRUE); if it is wrong, write F (FALSE).

1 A TNC is an organisation that controls assets in one or two countries.
2 There will be fewer TNCs if we include in the definition the possession of a minimum number of associated companies in a minimum number of host countries.
3 In 1977 there were 5,586 firms which operated in six or more host countries.
4 If the minimum size of the TNC expands (e.g. operating in more countries), so the share of American TNCs in the total will increase.
5 The UN has recommended that one all-purpose definition of TNCs should be used.

B   Write brief answers to the following questions, obtaining your information from the passage.

1 Give three examples of the kind of assets that TNCs control in a number of countries.
2 Give examples of criteria which will reduce the number of TNCs.
3 Complete the table below with as much information as you can.

Transnational corporations

criteria TNCs	*... with min. of 1 foreign affiliate*	*... in 2 or more host countries*	*... in 6 or more host countries*
Number of TNCs in 1977			
US TNCs % of total TNCs			

4 Apart from the items in the simplest definition of a TNC, what additional features could be included in a definition?

Exercise 1A

Alternative vocabulary

Below is a list of words (and line numbers) from the text (1–7). Next to them is a list of synonyms or explanations, in mixed order (a–g). Match the words from the text with their synonyms.

1 straightforward (1)   a similar
2 the like (3)   b put, placed
3 affiliate (5)   c simple
4 dominance (14)   d too much emphasis
5 by virtue of (14)   e associated company
6 undue stress (21)   f control, power, importance
7 laid (21)   g as a result of, because of

Exercise 1B
Explanation

In line 8 the term *host countries* is used. Can you explain its meaning as used in the text? Use a dictionary if necessary.

Language use

Exercise 1
More definitions

In Unit 1 Stage 1 we looked at some ways of writing definitions. Look again, quickly, at the examples of definitions in that unit (Language use, Exercise 2). Now look at the following definition from the Stage 1 text in this unit:

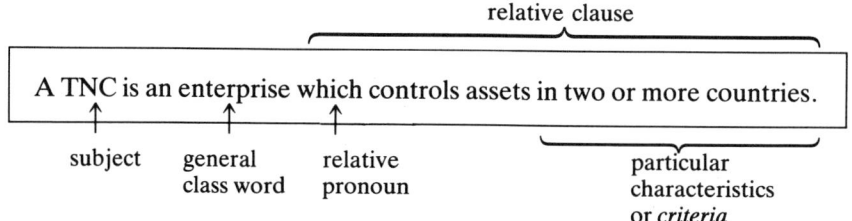

Such a definition will often include a list of characteristics or *criteria* and sometimes *examples*. Ways in which examples may be listed are looked at in the next exercise.

1 It is sometimes difficult to distinguish between the following words:

an affiliate, a company, a corporation, an enterprise, a firm, an industry

Look carefully at the following definitions. Use the appropriate word from the list above to complete each definition. If necessary use a dictionary.

a _____ is a basic production unit which carries on business and varies in size from a one-person business to a multinational organisation.

b _____ is an association of persons which is formed for the purpose of carrying on trade or business and has a separate identity from the persons who combine to form it.

c _____ is an associated company which is a subsidiary of a parent company.

d _____ is a collective term which is used to describe a business activity, usually large in size.

e _____ is a business organisation which has limited liability and has a legal existence separate from the persons who combine to form it. (*Note:* This term is normally used in the USA; in the UK the term 'limited company' is normally used.)

f _____ is a collective term which is used to describe a group of firms which operate in the same area of production.

2 Now write your own definitions of the following words, similar in style to those above.

a an asset
b a business
c a factory

Exercise 2
Exemplification

In the text in this stage, and also in the Stage 2 text, there are a number of instances of ways of giving examples (or exemplifying). Exemplification is often used in a subject like economics in order to help the understanding of a definition or an explanation, or to illustrate them. The following are some of the most common ways of indicating examples:

1 for example, . . .   (*Note: for example* may come after the item itself)
2 e.g., . . .
3 such as . . .
4 (. . ., . . ., . . .)   (*Note:* the examples are listed between brackets)
5 – . . ., . . ., . . . –   (*Note:* sometimes only the first dash is used)
6 A whole sentence may be an example of something from the previous sentence.
7 Examples of (such) . . . are . . .
8 Such . . . include (*or* are, etc.) . . .
9 for instance, *or* instances
10 illustrate, *or* illustration (*Note:* some uses of these only)

Note: Many of the examples above include lists of items. Such lists involve the use of commas (,) after each item and the use of *and/or* before the last item in the list.

Starting with the Stage 1 text and then proceeding, if necessary, to the Stage 2 text, give one example from the text of each of the first eight ways above of giving examples (give their stage and line references). Here is an example:

1 '*for example*, by exports or licensing arrangements' (Stage 2, line 34)

Now find another example of this type from Stage 1, and then examples of 2–8 above.

Open exercise

Compose five examples of different ways of giving examples similar to the ones you have written above. You can obtain the information you need from any of the previous units.

Exercise 3
Back reference

Words like *it*, *this* and *these* often refer to something earlier in the sentence or in a previous sentence. (Sometimes they refer forward to something following.) Decide what the following words refer to in the Stage 1 text. Give the reference (or subject) and the line number. Here is an example:

this (line 3) the most straightforward definition (of a TNC = an enterprise which controls assets in two or more countries). (lines 1–3)

1 *it* (line 2)   **3** *these* (line 14)
2 *these* (line 9)   **4** *their* (line 14)

Stage 2 Economic characteristics

Comprehension

Pre-questions

Before you read the passage, read the following questions. Do you know the answers already? Discuss them with other students to see if they know the answers. The questions will help to give a purpose to your reading; it is not necessary to write the answers.

1 What are the main economic sectors in which Transnational Corporations (TNCs) have a leading position?
2 What are the main advantages that TNCs have over local competitors?
3 What is the basic world-wide aim of the parent corporations of TNCs?

1 Large organisations engaged in international production are not a new phenomenon, but the actual forerunners of today's TNCs did not begin to emerge until the end of the nineteenth century, and their rapid expansion in LDCs has largely occurred in the post-Second World War period. The
5 attractiveness of TNCs to LDCs is that direct foreign investment (DFI) by the TNCs provides, in 'package' form, those resources otherwise not available to LDCs (technology, marketing skills) or only available in insufficient quantities (capital, enterprise).

TNC investment is heavily concentrated in a few LDCs. Ten countries
10 (Brazil, Mexico, India, Malaysia, Argentina, Singapore, Peru, Hong Kong, the Philippines and Trinidad and Tobago) accounted for 40 per cent of the stock of DFI in 1975, and if we add to this the share of members of OPEC

(Organisation of Petroleum Exporting Countries) and the tax havens
(countries such as the Bahamas, Bermuda and the Cayman Islands), the
15 combined share of these countries in total LDC DFI is 76 per cent.

TNCs have developed dominant positions in a number of productive
sectors in the LDCs. Traditionally, DFI was concentrated in the extractive
sectors (oil, copper, iron ore, bauxite) and plantation agriculture (rubber,
tea, sugar), but recent years have seen the rapid growth of DFI in the
20 services sector (banking, insurance, advertising, consultancy) and in
manufacturing. Within the latter sector, we can distinguish between
research-intensive, technologically advanced activities (pharmaceuticals,
chemicals, machinery and office equipment) and those activities where
product differentiation and marketing power are of greater importance
25 (foodstuffs, soft drinks, cosmetics, automobiles). The distinction is not
always a clear-cut one as much research and development expenditure (R
and D) is directed towards making minor product changes (in pharmaceuticals for example), rather than directed towards basic research and the
development of major new products and/or processes.
30 Clearly, TNCs invest in LDCs for a variety of reasons – access to raw
materials, utilisation of cheap labour (especially important in the case of
export-oriented activities) and supplying host country markets. But why
should the resources or the markets of LDCs be utilised via DFI rather
than, for example, by exports or licensing arrangements? For direct
35 investment to be profitable, most economists now accept the argument that
the TNC must possess some advantage which local competitors (assuming
that there are any) do not have access to. Examples of such *ownership-
specific advantages* are marketing skills, superior organisational skills and
management techniques, the ability to differentiate products, the owner-
40 ship or control of proprietary process technologies, etc. It is further argued
that the TNC can most profitably exploit its ownership-specific advantages
through DFI, rather than through the market (that is, rather than by selling
or licensing its technology or exporting its output). It is thus through what
has been termed the process of *internalising* its assets, rather than by selling
45 or licensing them to foreign producers, that the TNC can most fully profit
from its unique advantages. We must also take into account, however,
location-specific factors (relative costs of production, marketing factors,
trade barriers, government policies) to obtain a more complete understanding of the process of DFI, although obviously the relative importance of
50 such factors will vary according to the nature and objectives of each
individual act of DFI.

Three further points deserve brief mention. Firstly, it needs to be
emphasised that TNCs dominate in oligopolistic market structures (markets
effectively controlled by a few buyers or sellers), and that their behaviour
55 patterns can be analysed within an oligopoly framework. Oligopolists
compete with one another through product differentiation, advertising,
rapid technological innovation of both products and processes and through
competitive entry to LDC markets. TNCs create knowledge and, by

organising transactions within the firm itself, they ensure that, even when
60 they operate within different countries, the private returns to their
investment in information are fully appropriated by themselves.

Secondly, TNCs plan, organise and manage their operations on a global
scale, viewing the world as a single economic unit. It is the parent
corporation that determines corporate strategy, decides on the location of
65 new investment, allocates research programmes and export markets to
various parts of the corporation and determines the prices that are charged
on intra-corporate transactions (transfer prices).

Thirdly, it can be assumed that the maximisation of global profits is the
overall, long-term corporate objective, even though other theories of firm
70 behaviour (managerial and behavioural) may be useful in explaining TNC
behaviour in specific situations. To achieve this objective, TNCs have
devised a variety of financial strategies which attempt to minimise both the
risks they face and the taxes they pay, although these two objectives may
occasionally conflict. Such strategies include heavy reliance on the reinvest-
75 ment of profits and local borrowing to finance affiliate operations, the take-
over of existing firms rather than the establishment of new ones and the
manipulation of transfer prices in order to avoid tax payments, to by-pass
exchange control regulations or to minimise liabilities in weak currencies.

We noted above that DFI is concentrated in relatively few LDCs but this
80 does not mean that DFI is not important in other LDCs. Size is a relative
concept and even small TNCs, if concentrated in strategic, rapidly growing,
advanced technology sectors, can exert an influence which belies their
quantitative significance. TNCs are often 'market leaders' in the oligopol-
ised sectors of the LDC economy, and domestic firms are forced to become
85 'more like' TNCs if they are to survive and prosper.

In addition, data relating to the stock of DFI or the number of TNCs are
inadequate indicators of the extent of TNC activities and their influence in
LDCs. Non-equity operations, such as the licensing of technology, the use
of management and technical agreements and the utilisation of brand
90 names and trade marks, have become more common in recent years and the
United Nations (UN, 1978, Ch. 3) highlights their growth as an important
aspect of the continuing evolution of the TNC.

References and suggested reading

Colman, D. and Nixson F. (1978), *Econ-omics of Change in Less Developed Coun-tries*, Oxford, Philip Allan, Ch. 9.

Dunning, J. H. (1981), *International Pro-duction and the Multinational Enterprise*, London, George Allen & Unwin.

Hood, N. and Young S. (1979), *The Econ-omics of Multinational Enterprise*, London, Longman.

United Nations (1978), *Transnational Cor-porations in World Development: A Re-examination*, E/C.10/38, New York.

United Nations (1979), *Supplementary Ma-terial on the Issue of Defining Transnation-al Corporations*, E/C.10/58, New York.

Comprehension

Post-questions

After you have read the passage write brief answers to the following
questions. Try to express your answers in your own words if possible.

1 Why do LDCs generally welcome TNCs?

2 Which are the main groups of countries receiving direct foreign
investment?

3 What are the main reasons why TNCs invest in LDCs?

4 In order for TNCs to profit fully from their particular advantages in
LDCs, do they prefer DFI or selling and licensing their technology?

5 What are the main ways in which TNCs compete with each other or with
other big firms in their operations?

6 In order to achieve maximum profits, what are the main financial tactics
that TNCs often employ?

Word study

**Exercise 1A
Alternative vocabulary**

Below is a list of words (and line numbers) from the text (1–25). Next to
them is a list of synonyms or explanations, in mixed order (a–y). Match the
words from the text with their synonyms.

1 phenomenon (2)	a because
2 actual (2)	b gaining control
3 forerunner (2)	c privately owned patent or trademark
4 package (6)	d gives a false idea of
5 otherwise (6)	e unusual or remarkable fact or event
6 tax havens (13)	f real
7 ore (18)	g bring to bear, have
8 bauxite (18)	h in a different way; from different sources
9 distinguish (21)	i invention, new method
10 pharmaceuticals (22)	j the clay from which alumina comes and thence aluminium
11 cosmetics (25)	k something that prepares the way for something bigger or more important coming later
12 as (26)	
13 minor (27)	l face cream, lipstick etc: 'make-up'
14 via (33)	m avoid, get round
15 rather than (33)	n instead of
16 proprietary (40)	o countries where very low (or no) taxes are paid
17 unique (46)	p by means of, through
18 innovation (57)	q business dealings
19 transactions (59)	r the rock from which metal can be obtained
20 devised (72)	s medicinal drugs
21 take-over (75)	t a complete deal or proposal including all items
22 manipulation (77)	u management or control by influence
23 by-pass (77)	v understand the difference
24 exert (82)	w planned
25 belies (82)	x special
	y small, less important

Exercise 1B
Explanation

The following words are taken from the text (line numbers are given). Can you explain their meaning as used in the text? Use a dictionary if necessary.

1 extractive sectors (17)
2 product differentiation (24)
3 oligopoly (55)
4 weak currencies (78)
5 brand names and trade marks (89)

Language use

Exercise 1
Sequence: summary

The Stage 2 text has been summarised below in two ways. Firstly, a diagram has been used to outline the content of the first three paragraphs. Secondly, the remainder of the text (from line 30) has been summarised by several 'key' sentences – but they are shown in a mixed order.

1 Complete the diagram below using very few words.

Figure 7.1   TNC investment in LDCs (DFI)

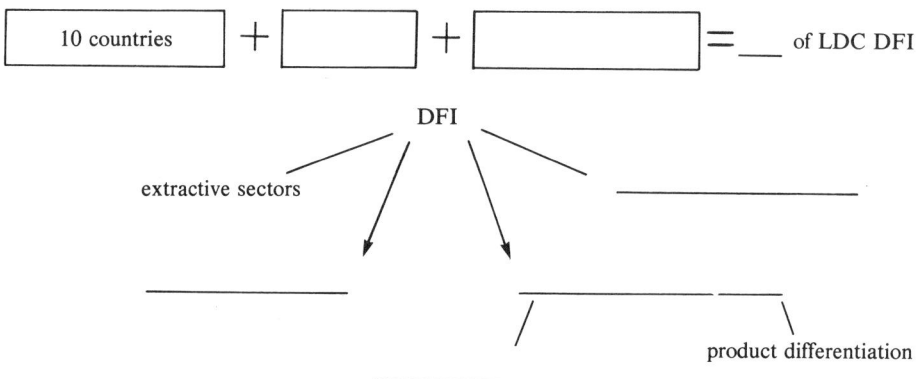

2 Rewrite the eleven mixed sentences in the correct sequence according to the meaning of the text.
   a DFI can be important in a number of LDCs, even if the TNC is small.
   b We must take into account location-specific factors.
   c TNCs invest in LDCs for a number of reasons.
   d TNCs organise their operations on a world-wide scale.
   e Non-equity operations have become increasingly important to TNCs.
   f Why should DFI be used instead of other arrangements?
   g It is by internalising its assets that the TNC can profit most from its special advantages.
   h If DFI is to be profitable, the TNC must possess ownership-specific advantages.
   i TNCs dominate in oligopolistic market structures.
   j The TNC can most profitably exploit these advantages through DFI.
   k The maximisation of world-wide profits is the long-term aim.

3 You will notice that all linking words and phrases have been omitted from the sentences above. Now write one paragraph with the above sentences in the correct order, joined together where necessary by appropriate linking words or phrases (e.g. *also*, *however*, etc.). Keep the same meaning as in the original text.

Extension activities

1 Writing: A case study

From your knowledge of the real world, and making use of books, journals or newspapers, as far as you are able to, write a description of the activities of one major TNC (e.g. Ford, Shell, IBM, Coca-Cola, ICI, Kodak, etc.). Try to give some idea of the product(s) with which the TNC is associated, the countries in which it operates, and the scale of its activities.

2 Group activity: Role-play – discussion

A transnational corporation
Working together in pairs if possible, students should consider the arguments for and against a TNC extending its operations to country X – a developing country.

One pair of students should imagine that they are the managers of a TNC. They should prepare arguments to try to persuade the government of a developing country (X) that it is in the interests of that country to allow the TNC to set up operations in that country. The managers can specify what their products are.

Another pair of students should imagine that they are members of the government of the developing country and that they are responsible for negotiating with the TNC. They should prepare some specific questions for the TNC, designed to maximise the benefits and minimise the costs to the host country.

The TNC should present its arguments (orally) which should be questioned by the LDC. Depending on the result of the arguments and answers to questions, the goverment team can decide whether or not it is in the interests of the LDC to allow the TNC to operate there. If other students are listening to the arguments, they could be allowed to ask questions as well and to vote at the end on whether or not the TNC should operate in the LDC.

Unit 8   Technology and development

Stage 1   What is technology?

1   Technology can be broadly defined as the 'skills, knowledge and procedures for making, using and doing useful things' (quoted in Stewart, 1977, p. 1). Technology thus defined includes both process technology (*how* something is made) and product technology (the nature and specification of *what* is
5   made). It also includes the whole range of managerial, organisational, financial and marketing skills which LDCs can obtain either through DFI or through the various non-equity arrangements referred to in Unit 7, Stage 2.

    Technology is an essential input to production and it can be acquired by LDCs, embodied in a variety of forms:

10   1 in capital goods, and sometimes intermediate goods, which are bought and sold in markets, usually in connection with investment decisions;

    2 in human labour, usually highly qualified and specialised manpower, with the capacity to make use of the equipment and techniques available;

    3 in information, of either a technical or commercial nature, which is
15   provided in markets or kept secret by those that own or control it (the latter is usually referred to as proprietary technology) (Dunning, 1982, p. 9).

However, the acquisition of technology poses a number of important problems for LDCs:

20   – Should they attempt to develop the required technologies for themselves or should they buy what they require in international markets?

    – If they decide to buy, is it best to acquire the technology as part of the DFI 'package' or is it preferable to obtain the technology through some other channel?

25   – Irrespective of the channel through which the technology is acquired, is the technology 'appropriate' with respect to the resource endowments and development objectives of the particular LDC?

    – What is the actual cost of the technology acquired by LDCs, either from TNCs or from other sources? Are LDCs paying 'too much' for the
30   technology they receive?

    – What policies should LDCs adopt to enable them to make better use of imported technologies and, in the longer run, to develop an indigenous technological capacity, that is, to be able to generate new technologies themselves?

35   Given the current state of knowledge, definitive answers cannot at present be given to these questions. Increased awareness of the issues involved is, however, leading to a more informed discussion of these problems and to the formulation of more effective policies with respect to technology transfer and development.

Comprehension

A   The following statements are based upon the information in the passage. If a statement is correct, write T (TRUE); if it is wrong, write F (FALSE).

1 A general definition of technology includes only process and product technology.

2 Technology can be acquired by LDCs in the form of capital goods or human labour only.

3 There are no problems involved for LDCs in acquiring technology.

4 It is stated that LDCs are paying too much for the technology that they receive.

5 Final and decisive answers cannot be given to the questions raised because not enough is known at present.

6 One result of being more aware of the issues involved in acquiring technology is to lead to the framing of better policies regarding technology transfer and development.

B   Write brief answers to the following questions, obtaining your information from the passage.

1 What is the difference between process and product technology?

2 Where can LDCs acquire the various managerial etc. skills that are referred to?

3 What is 'proprietary technology'?

4 If an LDC decides to buy technology, what further question is it necessary to ask?

5 In acquiring technology and deciding upon suitable policies to adopt, what results might LDCs hope for?

Word study

Exercise 1A
Alternative vocabulary

Below is a list of words (and line numbers) from the text (1–6). Next to them is a list of synonyms or explanations, in mixed order (a–f). Match the words from the text with their synonyms.

1 acquired (8)	a produce
2 channel (25)	b regardless of, without regard to, no matter which, not taking into account
3 irrespective of (25)	
4 endowments (26)	c decisive, final, conclusive
5 generate (33)	d gained, obtained, received
6 definitive (35)	e way, means
	f that which it is provided with, that it naturally has

Exercise 1B
Explanation

The following phrases are taken from the text (line numbers are given). Can you explain their meaning as used in the text? Use a dictionary if necessary.

1 capital goods (10)
2 intermediate goods (10)

Language use

Exercise 1
Question forms

A   Notice that the title of Stage 1 is a question and that the text contains a number of examples of questions. They can be divided into two broad categories:

1   those that begin with a question (or 'wh-') word:
   What? Which? Who? (Whom?) Whose? When? Where? Why? How?
   e.g. What is the cost of the technology?

2   those that begin with an auxiliary verb : there are 24 of these verb forms:

am are is	*was were*	*shall will*
should would	*have has had*	*may might*
do does did	*can could*	
must ought need	*dare used*	

   e.g. Is the technology appropriate?

B   Notice in both examples the word order, especially the position of the verb (compared with the position in a statement). Notice also how the different types of questions may be answered. Type (1) needs some information in the answer. Type (2) can be answered 'Yes' or 'No' (although a reason may also be added).

e.g. 1   What *is* the cost of the technology?   *Answer:* £250,000
         Statement: The cost of the technology *is* £250,000.

     2   *Is* the technology appropriate?   *Answer:* Yes (, it is).
                                                              No (, it isn't).

         Statement: The technology *is* appropriate.

C   When there is no auxiliary verb in the sentence (i.e. those 24 words listed in A2 above) then, in order to form a question, the appropriate tense/form of *do* can be used with the infinitive of the verb.

e.g. Technology includes both . . .   *Does* technology *include* both . . .?

The statements below are based upon sentences in the Stage 1 text. For each one write an appropriate question based on the statement.

e.g. Technology can be defined as the 'skills, knowledge. . . .' etc.

     What is technology?

or: What can technology be defined as?

1 Technology includes both process technology and product technology.
2 Technology is an essential input to production.
3 Technology can be acquired by LDCs in a variety of forms.
4 Capital goods are bought and sold in markets.
5 Human labour has the capacity to make use of the equipment and techniques available.
6 Some information is provided in markets.
7 The acquisition of technology poses a number of important problems for LDCs.
8 Definitive answers cannot at present be given to these questions.

Exercise 2
Questions: further practice

Below are given some answers based on possible questions about the information in the Stage 1 text. Compose suitable questions to go with the answers.

e.g. Question: *What is process technology?*
     Answer: How something is made.

1 The whole range of managerial, organisational, financial and marketing skills.
2 Through DFI.
3 In Unit 7, Stage 2.
4 No, it is kept secret by its owners.
5 Yes, it is leading to a more informed discussion of the problems.

Stage 2 The transfer of technology to LDCs

Comprehension

Pre-questions

Before you read the passage, read the following questions. Do you know the answers already? Discuss them with other students to see if they know the answers. The questions will help to give a purpose to your reading; it is not necessary to write the answers.

1 What does orthodox economic theory say regarding production techniques in LDCs?
2 What are some of the effects in LDCs of the introduction of TNC capital-intensive technologies?
3 Which product or process technologies are most 'appropriate' for LDCs?

1 Given the relatively labour-abundant, capital-scarce resource endowment of the majority of LDCs, and assuming that the market prices of the factors of production reflect social opportunity costs, orthodox economic theory argues that LDCs should select techniques of production that utilise most
5 intensively their relatively abundant factor (labour) and economise on the use of the scarce factor (capital).

This proposition can be illustrated using simple production theory. Given a production function for a particular product expressing output as a function of capital and labour, it is possible to draw isoquants (equal output
10 lines), such as YY in the diagram on p. 84, which indicate all combinations of the two inputs which can be used to produce any given level of output. The isocost, or equal input cost line, (AB) is determined by the ratio of the price of labour to the price of capital (P_l/P_k) and represents all combinations of capital and labour which have the same total cost. At the point of
15 tangency (u) between the isoquant and isocost line, output will be maximised given the cost constraint. Alternatively, for any given output level, costs are minimised at the point of tangency. Given the isocost line AB, Y units of output are produced using 0l units of labour combined with 0k units of capital.

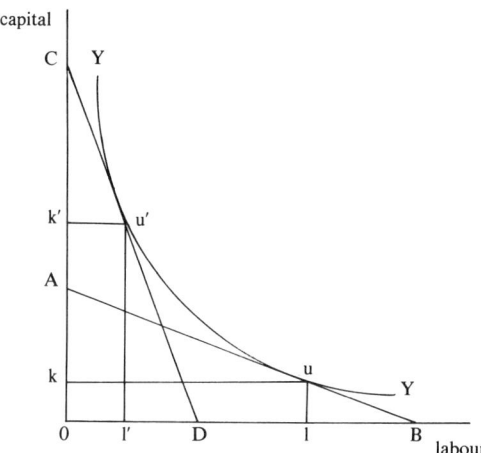

Figure 8.1

20   Common sense would, therefore, seem to dictate the choice of relatively labour-intensive techniques of production in relatively labour-abundant LDCs. The TNC, on the other hand, appears more likely to transfer capital-intensive technologies to the LDCs, technologies that have been developed in the relatively capital-abundant, labour-scarce industrialised economies.

25   Such technologies, it is argued, do not create large-scale new employment opportunities in the LDCs, they encourage a long-term dependence on imported machinery and equipment and associated inputs ('technological dependence'), and they slow down, or prevent, the effective anchorage and diffusion of the transferred technology in the host LDC.

30   A number of reasons have been advanced to explain the apparently inconsistent behaviour of TNCs in this respect. The neo-classical school, for example, argues that in the majority of LDCs, market prices do not reflect social opportunity costs. The price of labour is 'too high' (government minimum wage legislation, powerful trades unions), the price of capital is

35   'too low' (negative real interest rates, overvalued exchange rates) and thus both TNCs and national firms will tend to substitute 'cheap' capital for 'expensive' labour. It is also maintained that the lack of powerful competitive pressures in LDCs (arising largely through the restrictions placed on foreign competition via imports) lessens the need for firms to

40   minimise costs and become generally more efficient (see Unit 6, Stage 2 for further discussion of the neo-classical case).

Structuralist writers have tended to argue that there is only a limited possibility of substituting factors in the production process ('technical rigidity'). The distinction is made between:

45   1   the basic case in which, given the state of technical knowledge, there is only one (or at most only a few) manufacturing process(es) which is (are) capable of producing a given product;

2   technical rigidities related to the specifications of the commodity to be produced (an argument emphasised by Stewart, 1977);

50   3   technical rigidities imposed by the actual availability of techniques – even

if alternative techniques are available, LDCs may not have access to them (Forsyth *et al.*, 1980).

The choice of techniques controversy thus raises two crucial questions:

1 Is there a choice of technique in practice?

55 2 If a choice of technique does exist, do TNCs systematically employ more capital-intensive techniques than their indigenous (national) counterparts in LDCs?

The available empirical evidence is ambiguous and incomplete and does not permit definitive answers to be given to these questions. Econometric
60 estimates of factor substitutability vary significantly and are open to a number of objections (Morawetz, 1976). Similarly, various studies of matched pairs of TNCs and national firms (matched with respect to scale of output, product-mix, age of equipment and market conditions faced) reach conflicting results.

65 Overall, the evidence suggests that technical rigidity is in no sense complete and that both TNCs and national firms do in practice adapt to the conditions found in LDCs. Such adaptations are usually found in ancillary or peripheral operations (transport within the firm, packing, handling and storage operations), rather than in the 'core' manufacturing process. In
70 addition, there are important inter-industry variations in the degree of technical flexibility, with the possibilities for choosing between alternative techniques being greatest in long-established, basic industries, with low income elasticities of demand, catering for the needs of the mass of the population (clothing, food, household utensils, construction materials, etc.).

75 Perhaps more surprisingly, no systematic and consistent differences with respect to choice of technique are found between matched pairs of TNCs and local firms. This is possibly explained by the fact that in order to survive in the competitive struggle, national firms must become 'more like' TNCs with respect to product characteristics (quality, appearance), product
80 differentiation, advertising and so on.

What does emerge more clearly, however, is that TNCs are unlikely to become major suppliers of 'appropriate' product or process technologies to LDCs. 'Appropriate', in this context, usually means that the process technology is relatively labour-intensive and able to utilise locally available
85 raw materials and other inputs, the machinery and equipment is easy to maintain and repair and that the manufacturing enterprise's output can be scaled down to the smaller markets typical of LDCs. In addition, the product itself should, in some (not always clearly defined) sense, be 'appropriate' to the consumption requirements of the LDC.

90 The discussion in Unit 7, Stage 2 would lead us to conclude that the TNC is unlikely to possess, or be able to maintain, ownership-specific advantages with respect to the development of such processes or products. The need for the LDCs themselves, both individually and collectively, to formulate and implement realistic and effective policies to encourage indigenous tech-
95 nological development should thus be recognised and given high priority in the development effort.

References

Dunning, J. H. (1982), 'Towards a Taxonomy of Technology Transfer and Possible Impacts on OECD Countries', in OECD (1982), *North/South Technology Transfer: The Adjustments Ahead*, Paris.

Forsyth, D. J. C., McBain, N. S. and Solomon, R. F. (1980), 'Technical Rigidity and Appropriate Technology in Less Developed Countries', *World Development*, Vol. 8, No. 5/6, May/June, pp. 371–398.

Morawetz, D. (1976), 'Elasticities of Substitution in Industry: What Do We Learn from Econometric Estimates?', *World Development*, Vol. 4, No. 1, pp. 11–15.

Stewart, F. (1977), *Technology and Underdevelopment*, London, Macmillan.

Comprehension

Post-questions

After you have read the passage write brief answers to the following questions. Try to express your answers in your own words if possible.

1 In simple production theory, as exemplified in the diagram, what is an isoquant, and what does it show?

2 What is the significance of the point of tangency (u) in the diagram?

3 What is the main difference in emphasis between the neo-classical critics and structuralist critics regarding production in LDCs?

4 What kind of evidence is there to use in answering questions about choice of production techniques in LDCs?

5 Are there any big differences concerning choice of production techniques between TNCs and local firms in LDCs? What is the overall conclusion regarding the position of TNCs in LDCs?

Word study

Exercise 1A
Alternative vocabulary

Below is a list of words (and line numbers) from the text (1–16). Next to them is a list of synonyms or explanations, in mixed order (a–p). Match the words from the text with their synonyms.

1 reflect (3)	a	replacement
2 abundant (5)	b	fight, battle
3 dictate (20)	c	imprecise, unclear
4 anchorage (28)	d	supporting, subsidiary, secondary
5 advanced (30)	e	plentiful
6 inconsistent (31)	f	reduced
7 lessens (39)	g	securing, or making firm or stable
8 ambiguous (58)	h	prescribe, impose
9 substitutability (60)	i	illogical, contradictory
10 matched (62)	j	domestic implements, equipment or tools
11 adaptations (67)	k	comparative, counterpart, corresponding
12 ancillary (67)	l	reduces
13 core (69)	m	central
14 household utensils (74)	n	adjustments
15 struggle (78)	o	suggested, put forward
16 scaled down (87)	p	express, show

Exercise 1B
Explanation

The following words are taken from the text (line numbers are given). Can you explain their meaning as used in the text? Use a dictionary if necessary.

1 factors of production (2) **3** point of tangency (14)
2 ratio (12)   **4** consumption (89)

Language use

Exercise 1
Describing a diagram

A Look carefully at the second paragraph of the text which describes the diagram. Notice the language that is used in the description; in particular, notice the following constructions:

Given . . . it is possible to . . . such as . . .
X is determined by Y   For any given x, ⎫
At W . . . x will be y, given z Given x,   ⎬ y are z-ed
                                                           ⎭

B Look again at the diagram and at the description of it in the second paragraph. Make sure that you understand it.

1 Write a suitable general title for the diagram.
2 The following is a description of, and comment on, part of the diagram. Look carefully at the diagram, then complete the description below.

The line CD shows that the price of (1)_____ has fallen relative to (2)_____ . They are still producing the same amount of (3)_____ but producing it at (4)_____ using (5)_____ amount of capital and (6)_____ . In other words, cheaper capital has been substituted for (7)_____ .

Another way of explaining this is to say that the isocost line CD represents a higher relative wage, and results in the selection of a more (8)_____ production technique and a (9)_____ of employment (0l').

Extension activities

1 Writing: Essay
Near the end of the Stage 2 text (lines 88–90), when discussing the ability of TNCs to supply products to LDCs, there is the observation that 'the product itself should, in some sense, be "appropriate" to the consumption requirements of the LDC.' Discuss what you consider to be the consumption requirements of LDCs. Then give a list of several products that you consider are 'appropriate'. Justify your choice of products.

2 Group activity: Pyramid discussion
The procedure for conducting this activity is described on pages 7–8. Select from the list below what you consider to be the three most appropriate products for the consumption requirements of LDCs. The order of the three choices is not important.

1 beer	11 motor-cars
2 bicycles	12 personal computers
3 biscuits	13 shoes
4 bricks	14 soap
5 chewing gum	15 television
6 cigarettes	16 tinned (canned) fruit
7 Coca-Cola	17 tractors
8 cooking pots and pans	18 transistor radios
9 cosmetics	19 water-pumps
10 matches	20 wooden furniture

Unit 9 International trade and indebtedness

Stage 1 Trade and development

1   With political independence, the LDCs inherited a structure of production and international trade that had largely been designed to serve the interests of the metropolitan powers, rather than those of the LDCs themselves.

  They were heavily dependent on the production and export of a limited
5 range of primary commodities (foodstuffs, fuels and industrial raw materials) going mainly to the developed capitalist economies. In many cases, that dependence has not yet been broken. At the present time, for example, coffee still represents approximately 90 per cent of Burundi's recorded exports and 50 per cent of Colombia's; copper accounts for more than 70
10 per cent of Zambia's exports; cocoa represents more than 70 per cent of Ghana's exports. Many other examples could be given.

  The import structures of the LDCs were dominated by the importation of manufactured goods and intermediate inputs – durable consumer goods, machinery and transport equipment, chemicals, petroleum and so on. At
15 independence, most trade was with the colonial 'mother country'.

  Orthodox economists tended to argue that this structure of production and trade was consistent with the LDCs' comparative advantage and that they enjoyed significant gains from trade. The critics of this view, however, maintained that the gains from trade were more likely, for a variety of
20 reasons, to be appropriated by the developed capitalist economies. The unequal exchange thesis, espoused by some neo-Marxists, went further and suggested that trade was actually carried out at the expense of the LDCs, reproducing the conditions of underdevelopment and poverty.

  At the centre of the relationship between trade and development remains
25 the controversy concerning the long-term (i.e. secular)[1] behaviour of the terms of trade of the LDCs. The commodity, or net barter, terms of trade are the ratio of the unit price of exports to the unit price of imports ($\frac{Px}{Pm}$), and a deterioration in the index implies that a given volume of exports is exchanged for a smaller volume of imports.

30   The secular deterioration hypothesis is associated with the work of Hans Singer and Raul Prebisch. In its original form, it was based on the argument that in the developed economies strong trades unions could ensure that workers, rather than consumers, benefited from productivity gains, whereas in the LDCs, higher productivity led to lower prices, thus benefiting
35 consumers in the developed economies. Associated with, although formally separate from, such arguments was the view that primary commodity export prices were highly unstable and prone to violent fluctuations, thus damaging the development of the LDCs.

---

[1]*secular* = long-term trend; note also *cyclical* = short-term fluctuation around the long-term trend.

Comprehension

A The following statements are based upon the information in the passage. If a statement is correct, write T (TRUE); if it is wrong, write F (FALSE).

1 The structure of production and international trade that LDCs inherited when they became independent was generally to their advantage.

2 LDCs were greatly dependent on primary products for exports and on importing manufactured goods and intermediate inputs.

3 Some economists have agreed that LDCs have a comparative advantage in trade and have therefore benefited from it.

4 A worsening of the index of export and import prices for LDCs suggests that a smaller quantity of imports will be received in exchange for a given quantity of exports.

5 The secular deterioration theory was based on the argument that in the developed economies productivity gains benefited workers while in LDCs higher productivity benefited consumers in the developed economies.

6 The view was held that variations in the export prices of primary products were to the advantage of the LDCs.

B Write brief answers to the following questions, obtaining your information from the passage.

1 Give three examples of the current reliance of LDCs on primary products for exports.

2 What are the arguments which suggest that there were no advantages to be gained by LDCs from their structure of production and trade?

3 Give a definition of the net barter terms of trade.

Word study

**Exercise 1A
Alternative vocabulary**

Below is a list of words (and line numbers) from the text (1–9). Next to them is a list of synonyms or explanations, in mixed order (a–i). Match the words from the text with their synonyms.

1 indebtedness (title)	a exchange
2 serve the interests of (2)	b unsteady
3 durable (13)	c owing money
4 thesis (21)	d liable
5 espoused (21)	e theory
6 at the expense of (22)	f long-lasting
7 barter (26)	g supported, adopted
8 unstable (37)	h the advantage of, profit
9 prone (37)	i causing loss to, with the sacrifice of

**Exercise 1B
Explanation**

The following words are taken from the text (line numbers are given). Can you explain their meaning as used in the text? Use a dictionary if necessary.

1 durable consumer goods (13)
2 hypothesis (30)

Stage 2 Trade, the balance of payments and indebtedness

Comprehension

Pre-questions

Before you read the passage, read the following questions. Do you know the answers already? Discuss them with other students to see if they know the answers. The questions will help to give a purpose to your reading; it is not necessary to write the answers.

1 What was the export experience of LDCs during the 1970s?
2 What are the most important changes that have occurred in the structure of LDC exports from the mid-1950s onwards?
3 Have any groups of LDCs especially profited from international trade?

1   Table 9.1 gives a broad overview of the international trade experience of the LDCs in the post-war period. There was an increase in the rate of growth of export volume between the 1950s and the 1960s, but a marked fall in the rate of growth in the 1970s, largely owing to the reduction in the
5   volume of oil imports following the rise in oil prices. For the non-oil LDCs, the 1970s witnessed an acceleration in the rate of growth of export volume, but there was a fall in the purchasing power of exports owing to the deterioration in the terms of trade. The contrast between the experience of the fast growing exporters of manufactures and the least developed LDCs is
10   especially noteworthy.

TABLE 9.1   Foreign trade indicators for developing countries
(annual percentage rates of change)

	Export volume	Import volume	Purchasing power of exports	Terms of trade
All developing countries				
1948–1960	4.4	5.3	5.2	0.8
1960–1970	6.4	5.4	6.2	−0.2
1970–1980	3.1	7.3	10.0	6.8
Major oil exporters				
1960–1970	8.6	4.7	7.2	−1.3
1970–1980	−1.4	14.3	17.9	19.6
Non-oil exporting developing countries				
1960–1970	5.1	5.6	5.7	0.6
1970–1980	7.6	4.8	4.5	−2.9
Fast growing exporters of manufactures				
1960–1970	5.8	6.9	7.0	1.1
1970–1980	11.8	7.1	8.2	−3.2
Least developed countries				
1960–1970	4.4	5.5	3.6	−0.8
1970–1980	−0.4	1.5	−2.2	−1.8

Source: UNCTAD, *Trade and Development Report, 1981*, United Nations, New York,
Table 12, p. 38.

Table 9.2 gives data on the share of the major economic groupings in world trade. Between 1950 and 1972, there was a dramatic fall in the share of all LDCs in world trade, but this trend was reversed in 1973 with the increase in oil prices. The share of the least-developed LDCs continued to
15   fall, however.

TABLE 9.2 Share of major economic groupings in total world trade (by value) (percentages)

Grouping	Exports					Imports				
	1950	**1960**	**1970**	**1972**	**1980**	**1950**	**1960**	**1970**	**1972**	**1980**
World	*100.0*	*100.0*	*100.0*	*100.0*	*100.0*	*100.0*	*100.0*	*100.0*	*100.0*	*100.0*
Developed market-economy countries	61.1	66.8	71.3	71.8	63.3	65.3	65.9	72.3	72.7	69.6
Developing countries	30.8	21.5	18.1	17.8	28.1	26.7	22.2	17.1	16.5	21.5
Major oil exporters	6.2	6.8	6.2	6.9	16.2	4.1	4.6	3.3	3.7	6.5
Other developing of which:	24.6	14.9	11.7	10.9	11.9	22.6	17.6	13.8	12.9	15.0
Fast growing exporters of manufactures	7.8	3.9	3.4	3.6	4.9	7.3	4.9	4.3	4.5	5.8
Least developed	1.5	1.1	0.7	0.6	0.3	1.3	1.2	0.9	0.7	0.6
Socialist countries	8.1	11.7	10.6	10.4	8.6	7.9	11.9	10.5	10.1	9.0

Source: UNCTAD, *Trade and Development Report, 1981,* United Nations, New York, Annex Table A.4, p. 116

Of particular importance are the changes that have occurred in the structure of LDC exports in the post-war period. The data in Table 9.3 clearly show the doubling in the share in total exports of fuels and the three-fold increase in the share of manufactured goods (a phenomenon referred to in Unit 6, Stage 2). The shares of food and agricultural raw materials in
20   total exports have fallen significantly.

TABLE 9.3 The structure of LDC exports, selected years 1955–78 (percentages)

	1955	1960	1970	1978
Total exports	*100*	*100*	*100*	*100*
Food	36.5	33.6	26.5	16.4
Agricultural raw materials	20.5	18.3	10.0	4.8
Minerals, ores	9.9	10.6	12.3	4.6
Fuels	25.2	27.9	32.9	52.8
Manufactures	7.7	9.2	17.7	20.9
Total non-fuel exports	*100*	*100*	*100*	*100*
Food	48.9	46.7	39.5	34.8
Agricultural raw materials	27.4	25.3	14.9	10.1
Minerals, ores	13.3	14.6	18.3	9.7
Manufactures	10.4	12.8	26.4	44.4
Share of MDCs in exports of LDCs				
Total non-fuel exports	76.3	74.3	71.9	65.4
Food	79.0	77.7	74.0	65.6
Agricultural raw materials	74.3	67.8	64.4	61.8
Minerals, ores	94.5	92.0	89.2	78.0
Manufactures	45.9	54.0	61.2	63.3

MDC = more developed country   *Source:* Riedel (1984), Table 1, p. 60

Table 9.4 gives details of the overall balance of payments position of the LDCs. The main points to be noted relate to the deterioration in both the trade balance and the current account balance of the major oil exporters,

TABLE 9.4 Balance of payments summary of LDCs and territories, 1980–83, by major analytic groups (in billions of current dollars)

Region	Exports (f.o.b.)	Imports (f.o.b.)	Trade balance	Balance on non-factor services and private transfers	Investment income (net)	Current account balance	Total capital flows (net)	Changes in reserves (minus equals increases)
	1	2	3	4	5	6	7	8
Major oil exporters								
1980	311.5	135.5	175.9	−62.6	−0.9	112.4	−53.5	−58.9
1981	289.8	150.2	139.6	−68.6	5.8	76.8	−78.2	1.4
1982	238.2	163.8	74.4	−75.5	14.0	12.9	−32.3	19.3
1983	270.1	185.6	84.5	−86.4	12.8	12.8	−7.9	−3.0
Other oil exporters								
1980	41.8	47.1	−5.3	2.0	−8.4	−11.7	14.4	−2.7
1981	43.5	53.7	−10.2	0.2	−11.8	−21.8	22.8	1.0
1982	45.3	53.7	−8.4	3.9	−15.8	−20.3	21.0	−0.7
1983	51.6	59.4	−7.8	4.3	−16.8	−20.3	21.2	−0.9
Net oil-importing countries								
1980	200.9	251.8	−50.9	8.7	−22.2	−64.8	56.7	8.1
1981	212.9	259.9	−47.1	9.7	−32.7	−70.1	61.5	8.6
1982	228.1	271.0	−42.9	11.0	−38.1	−70.0	68.3	1.7
1983	260.0	302.7	−42.7	12.8	−42.6	−72.4	74.1	−1.6
Exporters of manufactures								
1980	113.2	132.5	−19.3	5.9	−14.9	−28.3	23.9	4.2
1981	130.2	141.8	−11.6	7.1	−22.1	−26.6	26.3	0.3
1982	140.9	148.2	−3.2	7.2	−24.8	−24.9	27.3	−2.4
1983	161.8	167.9	−6.1	8.0	−26.5	−24.5	27.1	−2.6
MSA countries								
1980	34.8	53.7	−18.9	4.5	−2.3	−16.7	14.8	1.9
1981	31.7	53.1	−21.4	4.6	−3.4	−20.2	17.2	3.0
1982	33.6	55.0	−21.5	4.8	−4.1	−20.7	20.0	0.7
1983	37.7	61.4	−23.7	5.1	−5.0	−23.6	24.2	−0.6
Least developed countries								
1980	6.7	13.6	−6.9	0.5	−0.1	−6.5	5.5	1.0
1981	6.2	13.3	−7.1	0.8	−0.6	−6.9	7.4	−0.5
1982	6.7	14.0	−7.3	1.0	−0.9	−7.2	7.5	−0.3
1983	7.9	15.5	−7.6	1.2	−1.1	−7.5	7.9	−0.4

MSA = most severely affected, a group of the poorest LDCs, including most of those classified as least developed, which have been *most severely affected* by adverse international conditions

Note: 1981 figures are preliminary; 1982–83 figures are forecasts.

Source: UNCTAD, *Trade and Development Report, 1982*, United Nations, New York, Annex Table A.4.B, p. 131

Notes
columns 1, 2, 3 = visible items
columns 4, 5 = invisible items
column 5 = DFI
column 6 = visible and invisible
columns 6 + 7 = column 8

Column 4
non-factor services = includes payments for freight and insurance, and investment income other than on account of DFI.

private transfers = migrants' transfers and workers' remittances

25 the growing current account deficits of all other LDCs (although the exporters of manufactured goods have reduced their current account deficits), and the increasing dependence of the majority of the LDCs on capital inflows of various kinds to restore short-term equilibrium in their balance of payments.

30 Although the LDCs in general succeeded in financing successively larger current account deficits, a number of problems arose in the 1980s. During the 1970s, the LDCs' medium- and long-term debt increased by 20 per cent per annum, but the resources needed to service the debts also grew rapidly. The total amount of long-term external debt increased significantly but, in 35 general, a 'debt problem' was not perceived.

Since 1980, however, although the rate of growth of debt has halved, the reduction in the rate of growth of export earnings has been even greater and the ratio of debt to exports has risen significantly (World Bank, 1983, p. 21). In addition, higher interest rates have raised the ratio of debt service 40 obligations to exports. More than twenty LDCs have been forced to negotiate the rescheduling of their debts since 1980 (World Bank, 1983, p. 22).

The international trade and payments position of the LDCs is thus complex, and the temptation to generalise must be resisted. The belief 45 widely held in the late 1950s and early 1960s that trade could no longer be regarded as an 'engine of growth' for the LDCs was clearly based on a too pessimistic and over-simplified analysis of the possibilities of trade for the LDCs. Many LDCs (the major oil exporters and the NICs in particular) have obviously derived great benefit from trade and it has proved to be a 50 dynamic element in their development process. Other LDCs, on the other hand, for example, the economies of sub-Saharan Africa, have yet to change radically their structures of production and trade and participate more fully in the rapidly evolving 'new international division of labour'.

References

Riedel, J. (1984), 'Trade as the Engine of Growth in Developing Countries, Revisited', *Economic Journal*, Vol. 94, No. 373, March, pp. 56–73.

World Bank (1983), *World Development Report, 1983*, World Bank, Washington D.C.

Comprehension

Post-questions

After you have read the passage write brief answers to the following questions. Try to express your answers in your own words if possible.

1 Was there any difference in the export situaton of non-oil LDCs in the 1970s compared with the 1960s? If so, what was it?

2 What were the main differences between the least-developed LDCs and all LDCs in their share of world exports between 1950 and 1980?

3 What differences were there between the shares of food and fuels in LDC total exports from 1955 to 1978?

4 What were the main changes in the import and export situation of exporters of manufactured goods between 1980 and 1983?

5 What was the background to the 1980s debt problems of LDCs?

6 Has trade been an 'engine of growth' for all LDCs since the 1960s?

Word study

Exercise 1A
Alternative vocabulary

Below is a list of words (and line numbers) from the text (1–15). Next to them is a list of synonyms or explanations, in mixed order (a–o). Match the words from the text with their synonyms.

1 overview (1)	a	observed, recognised
2 witnessed (6)	b	take part in
3 reversed (13)	c	reorganisation of repayment timetable
4 doubling (18)	d	general survey
5 equilibrium (28)	e	gloomy, expecting the worst
6 successively (30)	f	desire
7 perceived (35)	g	developing
8 halved (36)	h	saw
9 obligations (40)	i	one after another, following without interruption
10 negotiate (41)	j	completely altered, changed direction
11 rescheduling (41)	k	balance
12 temptation (44)	l	discuss and arrange
13 pessimistic (47)	m	become twice as many, increase by two times
14 participate (52)	n	requirements, agreements, repayments
15 evolving (53)	o	lessened or cut by half

Exercise 1B
Explanation

The following phrases are taken from the text (line numbers are given). Can you explain their meaning as used in the text? Use a dictionary if necessary.

1 the post-war period (17)
2 fuel (18)
3 to service the debts (33)

Language use

Exercise 1
Commenting on data
(tables)

A   There are several references in the text to dates and periods of time. They are given below in a summary together with their meaning. Notice how they are used in the text.

the post-war period = after 1945 (*Note:* the *pre*-war period would be before 1939.)

the 1950s (or the '50s)	= 1950–1959
the early 1950s (or the early '50s)	= 1950–1953
the mid-1950s	= 1954–1956
the late 1950s	= 1957–1959

The same way of referring to periods of years can, of course, be used for other *decades* (= periods of 10 years), e.g. 1960s, 1970s, etc.

B When commenting on data (in tables, graphs, etc.) reference is often made to the *upward* or *downward trend* of the figures, and attention is frequently drawn to significant items (... *as much/many/high/large as* ... = positive; ... *only* ... = negative). Below are shown some of the ways of describing data.

1

to	rise increase grow - - - - - fall decline drop	slightly slowly gradually steadily steeply sharply rapidly suddenly dramatically significantly

2

a	slight small gradual steady marked big dramatic steep sharp rapid sudden significant	rise increase growth - - - - - fall drop reduction decline decrease

Note: In the two tables above some of the adjectives/adverbs (e.g. *slight/ slightly*) are more likely than others to be used with certain nouns or verbs.

3 The following words and phrases are also used when describing data:

to fluctuate/a fluctuation	to remain constant ...
to accelerate/an acceleration	to reach a peak in/at/of ...
to improve/an improvement	to level off (at) ...
to deteriorate/a deterioration	

C Notice the following expressions for indicating magnitude when comparing quantities, amounts, percentages, numbers, etc.

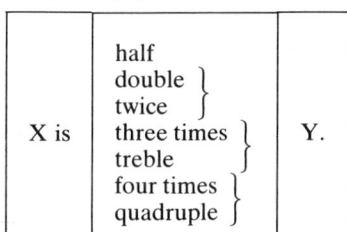

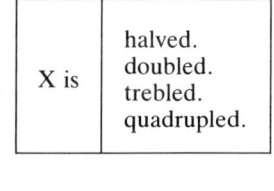

D When commenting on data it is often necessary to make comparisons. This is frequently done by using **linking words** or **connectives** that indicate a **contrast**. Of these, the two most common ones are *but* and *however*. Others that are often used are: *although*, *on the other hand*, *whereas*, *while*. These are shown below in examples taken from this unit. Notice how the words are used.

1 There was an increase ... between the 1950s and the 1960s, *but* a marked fall ... in the 1970s.
2 ... there was a dramatic fall in the share of all LDCs in world trade, *but* this trend was reversed in 1973 ... The share of the least-developed LDCs continued to fall, *however*.
Note: However often appears at the beginning of a sentence, linking it to the previous one (e.g. *However*, the share of ...) or it may appear after the introductory element in a sentence that is to be contrasted e.g. Since 1980, *however*, ...

3 *Although* the LDCs in general succeeded in . . ., a number of problems arose . . .
4 Many LDCs have obviously derived great benefit from trade . . . Other LDCs, *on the other hand* . . . have yet to change radically their structures of production . . .
5 . . . in the developed economies strong trades unions could ensure that workers . . . benefited from productivity gains, *whereas* (or *while*) in the LDCs, higher productivity led to lower prices, *thus* (or *therefore*) benefiting consumers in the developed economies.

E   Now follows some practice in using Tables 9.1–4. Where appropriate use any of the vocabulary and language constructions shown above.

1 *Table 9.1*
In the text it says that 'the contrast between the experience of the fast growing exporters of manufactures and the least developed LDCs is especially noteworthy.' (lines 8–10) Describe the relevant parts of the data that provide evidence for this statement.

2 *Table 9.2*
  a Looking at the developing countries' exports, contrast the position of the 'major oil exporters' with 'other developing countries'.
  b Comment on the trade trend of the socialist countries.

3 *Table 9.3*
Comment on the share of more developed countries (MDCs) in the exports of LDCs.

4 *Table 9.4*
The text describes the main trends in the table (lines 22–29). The main points are listed below. Find the appropriate data from the table that illustrate these points.
  a 'the deterioration in both the trade balance and the current account balance of the major oil exporters'
  b 'the growing current account deficits of all other LDCs'
  c 'the exporters of manufactured goods have reduced their current account deficits'
  d 'the increasing dependence of the majority of the LDCs on capital inflows of various kinds to restore short-run equilibrium in their balance of payments'

Extension activities

1 Writing: Essay
Select either your own country or one whose economy you have some knowledge of. Make use of any relevant books, articles, etc. Describe the trend of the country's exports since 1945, both in value and in structure. Comment, as far as you can, on the overall trade and balance of payments position of the country.

2 Group activity: Discussion
World trade in the year 2000
Individually, or in pairs, prepare to take part in a discussion on world trade in the year 2000. Try to predict what the position will be for *exporters of manufactures* and *least developed countries*. Refer to Tables 9.1–4 for the basis of your predictions. Also make use of your knowledge of the real world. If necessary, make intelligent guesses! Be prepared to justify your predictions with evidence or reasons.

Unit 10   Inflation

Stage 1 The inflationary experience of LDCs

1 Inflation is defined as a persistent rise in the general level of prices (or, alternatively, as a persistent fall in the purchasing power of money). A rise in a particular price is not inflationary if it is offset by falls in other prices, and a once-and-for-all rise in prices (owing, for example, to harvest failure)
5 will not be inflationary unless it is accompanied by responses that turn it into a process (an inflationary spiral) over time. The latter point highlights the importance of the transmission or propagating mechanism, discussed in greater detail in Stage 2.

That inflation is a problem for the majority of LDCs is clearly
10 demonstrated by the data presented in Table 10.1. For the non-oil

TABLE 10.1 Developing countries – changes in consumer prices, 1968–81 (percentages)

	Average 1968–72[1]	Change from preceding year								
		1973	1974	1975	1976	1977	1978	1979	1980	1981
Oil exporting countries										
Weighted average [2]	8.0	11.3	17.0	18.8	16.8	15.5	10.2	10.5	12.6	13.1
Non-oil developing countries										
Weighted average	—	—	—	—	—	23.0	20.0	24.7	32.1	31.4
excluding China	9.1	22.1	28.7	27.0	27.6	27.0	23.6	29.0	36.9	37.2
By analytical group										
Weighted averages[2]										
Net oil exporters	4.1	11.1	20.6	14.6	14.9	22.8	17.7	17.7	24.2	24.6
Net oil importers	—	—	—	—	—	23.0	20.3	25.8	33.3	32.4
excluding China	10.0	24.1	30.2	29.4	30.2	27.9	24.8	31.2	39.3	39.7
Major exporters of manufactures	14.1	21.3	24.9	40.1	55.8	40.9	37.3	44.6	54.3	62.2
Low-income countries	—	—	—	—	—	7.1	3.7	6.8	11.6	9.6
excluding China	6.5	21.9	30.2	11.9	−0.1	11.2	6.5	11.5	15.9	17.6
Other net oil importers	8.4	31.9	40.3	29.1	19.7	20.5	19.3	24.6	32.9	20.2
By area										
Weighted averages[2]										
Africa	4.6	9.7	15.4	15.0	14.9	19.3	15.2	19.2	19.3	22.7
Asia	—	—	—	—	—	5.8	3.7	6.5	12.6	9.9
excluding China	6.5	21.5	30.3	10.2	0.3	7.8	5.7	9.4	16.0	15.4
Europe	6.1	12.7	17.5	14.7	12.5	16.2	21.1	27.5	40.5	25.9
Middle East	4.2	12.1	22.1	21.6	19.1	19.6	21.1	25.8	42.7	32.8
Western hemisphere	15.3	32.1	37.5	52.0	66.2	51.2	42.4	49.6	58.3	65.7

[1]Compound annual rates of change.
[2]Geometric averages of country indices, weighted by the average US dollar value of GDPs over the previous three years. (Geometric mean = calculated as the nth root of the product of n numbers e.g. geometric root of 1 and 4 = $\sqrt{1 \times 4}$ = $\sqrt{4}$ = 2.)

Source: International Monetary Fund, *Annual Report, 1982,* Washington D.C., Table 3, p. 13.

developing countries, excluding the People's Republic of China, inflation accelerated throughout the 1970s and continued to rise in 1980 and 1981. The major exporters of manufactured goods also experienced high rates of inflation, influenced partly by the inclusion in that group of Argentina and
15 Brazil, countries that traditionally seem to suffer from high rates of price increase.

Regional variations are also of significance. The Latin American (western hemisphere) economies suffer the highest rates of inflation, followed some way behind by the Middle East. Until the mid-1970s, inflation had never
20 been a pressing problem for the majority of African economies, but that situation changed then, partly as a consequence of the oil-price rises of 1974–76 and 1979–80.

All data from LDCs should be treated with caution, but special care should be exercised with respect to price data. The consumer price index
25 (cost of living index) may well have a pronounced urban bias and the wholesale price index may well be heavily weighted by the prices of imports and exports. Data availability and reliability are thus major problems inhibiting the study of inflationary process in LDCs.

Comprehension

A   The following statements are based upon the information in the passage. If a statement is correct, write T (TRUE); if it is wrong, write F (FALSE).

1 Inflation is defined as a persistent rise in the purchasing power of money.
2 It is not inflationary if a rise in one price is compensated for by falls in other prices.
3 A once-and-for-all rise in prices can never be inflationary.
4 The Middle East experienced the second highest rates of inflation.
5 Most African countries did not suffer from serious inflation until the mid-1970s.
6 It is very difficult to obtain dependable price data from LDCs and this causes serious problems when trying to study inflation in LDCs.

B Write brief answers to the following questions, obtaining your information from the passage and Table 10.1.

1 What is the difference between a price rise and an inflationary spiral? (You may need to check in the Glossary.)
2 What was one of the reasons for high rates of inflation among major exporters of manufactured goods?
3 Between 1968 and 1972:
   a Which groups had the highest compound annual average rate of change in consumer prices?
   b Which group had the lowest?
   c Which area showed the highest average?
4 Did all parts of the world experience similar rates of inflation between 1973 and 1981?
5 **a** Which part of the world had the lowest rate of inflation up to 1981?
   b Which group of companies experienced the lowest rate of inflation up to 1981?
6 Is there any evidence in Table 10.1 to suggest that China had a low rate of inflation (or lower than most countries)?

Word study

Exercise 1A
Alternative vocabulary

Below is a list of words (and line numbers) from the text (1–6). Next to them is a list of synonyms or explanations, in mixed order (a–f). Match the words from the text with their synonyms.

1	persistent (1)	a	reproduction
2	transmission (7)	b	applied, employed, taken
3	propagating (7)	c	urgent
4	inclusion (14)	d	continual
5	pressing (20)	e	containing, adding, putting
6	exercised (24)	f	passing on

Exercise 1B
Explanation

The following phrases are taken from the text (line numbers are given). Can you explain their meaning as used in the text? Use a dictionary if necessary.

1 an inflationary spiral (6)   2 wholesale price (26)

Language use

Exercise 1
Commenting on data
(continued)

In Unit 9 Stage 2 (Language use Exercise 1) we looked at ways of commenting on data. This exercise gives further practice in interpreting data.

1 Find the appropriate data from Table 10.1 that illustrate the following comments:
  a 'For the non-oil developing countries, excluding the People's Republic of China, inflation accelerated throughout the 1970s and continued to rise in 1980 and 1981.'
  b 'The major exporters of manufactured goods also experienced high rates of inflation.'
  c 'The Latin American (western hemisphere) economies suffer the highest rates of inflation, followed some way behind by the Middle East.'
  d 'Inflation had never been a pressing problem for the majority of African economies, but that situation changed in the mid-1970s.'

2 Briefly comment on the data for Asia, excluding China, in Table 10.1. Then compare these data with those for Europe.

Stage 2   The causes of inflation in LDCs

Comprehension

Pre-questions

Before you read the passage, read the following questions. Do you know the answers already? Discuss them with other students to see if they know the answers. The questions will help to give a purpose to your reading; it is not necessary to write the answers.

1 What are the basic differences between the structuralist and monetarist explanations of inflation?
2 Have changes in the international economy influenced inflation in LDCs since the mid-1970s?
3 Of what significance is inflation in affecting the distribution of income?

1   The explanation of inflation has always generated controversy in the economics profession – between demand-pull and cost-push theorists, between monetarists and various 'Keynesian' economists and, in the context of LDCs, between monetarists and structuralists.

5   The orthodox explanation of inflation is usually presented in terms of aggregate demand and aggregate supply curves. In Figure 10.1, an increase in aggregate demand from D_1D_1 to D_2D_2 will raise output and capacity utilisation, from Y_1 to Y_2. An increase in aggregate demand from D_2D_2 to D_3D_3 will further raise output (to Y_3) but will also raise prices (from P to

10   P_x). Given that the aggregate supply curve becomes vertical at Y_3 level of ouput, any further increase in aggregate demand (for example, to D_4D_4) will merely raise prices (to P_y) (for a further discussion, see Killick, 1981, Ch. 7).

Figure 10.1 Aggregate demand and aggregate supply curves

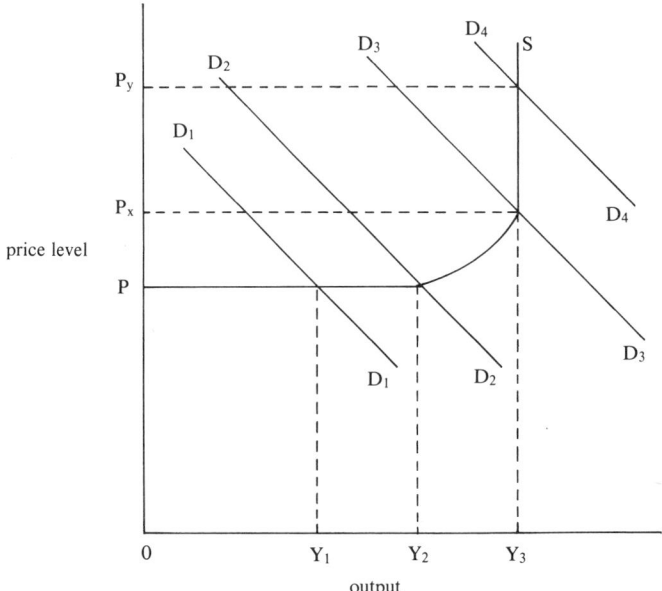

The Latin American structuralists rejected this theoretical framework,
15   and argued (as noted in Unit 3, Stage 2) that the LDC economy was characterised by a variety of market imperfections and rigidities, factor immobilities and sectoral disequilibria – underutilisation of productive capacity in some sectors co-existed with chronic shortages in others. For the structuralists, inflation was inevitable in an economy that was attempting to
20   grow rapidly in the presence of these various structural bottlenecks or constraints.[1]

The three bottlenecks usually identified are:

1 the agricultural sector bottleneck – urbanisation and rising incomes have led to rapidly rising demands for foodstuffs which cannot be met
25   by the agricultural sector (because, for example, of the structure of land ownership);

2 the foreign exchange bottleneck – the rate of growth of total foreign exchange receipts is not sufficient to finance the rate of growth of imports required in order to achieve some given, target rate of growth
30 of income (structural factors restrict the opportunities for the substitution of domestic for foreign resources);
3 the budget deficit bottleneck – rapid urbanisation and industrialisation place demands on government expenditure which cannot be met by increased revenue (because, for example, of the government's inability
35 to reform the tax system). The subsequent resort to deficit financing adds to the inflationary spiral.[2]

The monetarist, in contrast to the structuralist, sees inflation as a purely monetary phenomenon, the control of which requires as a necessary and sufficient condition the control of the money supply such that it grows at a
40 rate consistent with the growth of demand for money at stable prices. It is argued that there exists a stable demand function for real money balances. If the supply of money is greater than the demand for money, people have more money than they wish to hold and they will thus increase their expenditure. Output and/or prices will thus rise, depending on where the
45 economy is in relation to full employment output (in monetarist terminology, the 'natural' rate of unemployment).

Monetarists do not deny the existence of constraints or bottlenecks in the LDC. But, contrary to the structuralist assertion that such constraints are structural in nature, they argue that they are the result of price and
50 exchange rate distortions which are generated by inflation itself and government attempts to reduce the rate of price increase (price controls of foodstuffs, overvalued exchange rates, import controls, etc.). The structuralist causal relationship is thus reversed by the monetarist and it is argued that the bottlenecks in the economy constraining growth will be
55 eliminated when inflation itself is brought under control.
The discussion of the causes of inflation in the LDCs in the 1950s and 1960s took place largely within a stable international environment. The 1970s saw major changes in that environment including the collapse of the Bretton Woods system, massive increases in world liquidity and extensive
60 borrowing by a number of LDCs (see Unit 9, Stage 2), large increases in the price of oil and a limited number of other commodities and a cycle of boom, recession, recovery and further recession. Some economists (for example, Seers, 1981) have argued that a 'structuralist' theory of global inflation is required. Others (for example, Harberger, 1980) have analysed the
65 problem in terms of the global demand for, and the global supply of, money.
Econometric testing of the two competing hypotheses has in the past tended to favour the monetarist explanation of inflation in LDCs. This is not surprising given the close correlation that we would expect to find
70 between the rate of growth of money supply and the rate of growth of prices. Correlation does not imply causation, however, and most structuralists would argue that changes in the money supply are merely a passive or

permissive factor in the inflationary process, that is, an increase in the supply of money may well be a necessary condition for prices to rise, but it
75 is not a sufficient condition. In more formal terms, the structuralist would argue that money supply is determined endogenously rather than exogenously.

Structuralist hypotheses are very difficult to test empirically. The structural bottleneck is an *ex ante* concept, a gap that must be filled *ex post*
80 (for example, the *ex ante* demand for foreign exchange may be greater than the supply of foreign exchange, but in reality all imports are paid for and the *ex post* gap is closed). Proxy variables have usually to be used to test for the existence of structural constraints, and the results have rarely been satisfactory.

85 The so-called real activity model has been tested for a number of countries. It is based on the Phillips curve[3] but with the unemployment variable replaced by an indicator of excess demand in the goods market (the percentage deviation of output from potential output = GAP). The equation is as follows:

90
$$\dot{P}_t = b_0 + b_1 \, \text{GAP}_t + b_2 \, \dot{P}_t^e \tag{1}$$

where: $\dot{P}_t$ = percentage change in prices

$\dot{P}^e$ = price expectations

GAP_t = excess demand measure

Allowing for lagged effects, the equation becomes:

95
$$\dot{P}_t = b_0 + b_1 \, \text{GAP}_t + b_2 \, \text{GAP}_{t-1} + b_3 \, \dot{P}_t^e \tag{2}$$

This equation does not always perform well but the results are improved when structural variables are added:

$$\dot{P}_t = b_0 + b_1 \, \text{GAP}_t + b_2 \, \text{GAP}_{t-1} + b_3 \, \dot{P}_{t-1} + b_4 \, \dot{P}_r + b_5 \, \dot{P}_m \tag{3}$$

where: $\dot{P}_r$ = percentage change in relative food prices

100 $\dot{P}_m$ = percentage change in import prices

$\dot{P}_{t-1}$ = adaptive price expectations represented by lagged inflation rate.

In various tests of this model, the import price variable has a high and positive coefficient and the price expectations variable is also significant.
105 Rises in import prices thus appear to have played an important role in the 1970s in fuelling inflationary pressures in many LDCs.

The major problem with this kind of model, especially when it is applied on a cross-country basis (as in Bhalla, 1981) is that it ignores the internal structures of LDCs and differences in those structures between LDCs. The
110 susceptibility of an LDC to imported inflationary pressures depends, *inter alia*, on the level and characteristics of its development, its natural resource endowment, its development and industrialisation strategies and the structure and composition of its imports (which result from the previous factors). The problem remains, therefore, of identifying the most important
115 constraints, quantifying them, relating them to the level and strategy of development chosen and, ultimately, constructing a genuine structuralist

model of inflation, not merely adapting a monetarist model by the addition of a few proxy variables for structural factors.

120 A final point needs to be made. Inflation will almost certainly affect the distribution of income. The functional distribution may be affected by a redistribution from wages to profits and both the inter- and intra-sectoral distributions may be similarly affected (perhaps from agriculture to industry and, within industry, from 'old' to 'new' activities). Some social scientists have thus advanced an explanation of inflation in terms of the social conflict 125 that it generates over the distribution of the social product between different groups or classes. Redistribution is thus in an important sense a part of the propagation mechanism that keeps the inflationary spiral going. The real income of one group or class is eroded by inflation, it fights to restore its previous position and in turn passes on cost or price rises to other 130 groups that must similarly retaliate to maintain their own position. As Hirschman (1981, p. 201) remarked, inflation is indeed a remarkable invention that enables society to exist in a situation that is intermediate between extremes of social harmony and civil war!

---

[1] A structural bottleneck has been defined by Thorp (1971, p. 185) as a fundamental facet of the economic, institutional and socio-political structure of the economy which in one way or another inhibits the expansion of output.

[2] For a more detailed discussion of the structuralist case, see Kirkpatrick and Nixson (1976). The three bottlenecks discussed in the text are sometimes termed 'basic inflationary pressures' to distinguish them from 'exogenous inflationary pressures' (for example, a bad harvest, an increase in import prices) and the propagating mechanism, of which the budget deficit is an important component. See Sunkel, 1960.

[3] The original Phillips curve postulated an inverse correlation between the rate of wage inflation and the rate of unemployment (taken as a measure of excess demand or capacity utilisation). It was subsequently modified to take into account the fact that it is real wages, and not money wages, that both sides in the labour market attempt to influence, and thus price expectations must be incorporated into the relationship.

References

Bhalla, S. S. (1981), 'The Transmission of Inflation into Developing Economies' in W. R. Chine and Associates, *World Inflation and the Developing Countries*, Washington D.C., Brookings Institution.

Harberger, A. C. (1980), 'A Primer on Inflation' in W. L. Coats, Jr., and D. R. Khatkhate (eds.), *Money and Monetary Policy in Less Developed Countries: A Survey of Issues and Evidence*, Oxford, Pergamon Press.

Hirschman, A. O. (1981), 'The Social and Political Matrix of Inflation: elaborations on the Latin American experience' in *Essays in Trespassing: Economics to Politics and Beyond*, Cambridge, Cambridge University Press.

Killick, Tony (1981), *Policy Economics: A Textbook of Applied Economics on Developing Countries*, London, Heinemann.

Kirkpatrick, C. H. and Nixson, F. I. (1976), 'The Origins of Inflation in Less Developed Countries: A Selective Review' in M. Parkin and G. Zis (eds.), *Inflation in Open Economies*, Manchester, Manchester University Press; reprinted in I. Livingstone (ed.) (1981), *Development Economics and Policy: Readings*, London, Allen and Unwin.

Seers, D. (1981), 'Inflation: A Sketch for a Theory of World Inflation', *IDS Discussion Paper*, DP 169.

Sunkel, O. (1960), 'Inflation in Chile: an unorthodox approach', *International Economic Papers*, No. 10.

Thorp, R. (1971), 'Inflation and the Financing of Economic Development' in K. Griffin (ed.), *Financing Development in Latin America*, London, Macmillan.

Comprehension

Post-questions

After you have read the passage write brief answers to the following questions. Try to express your answers in your own words if possible.

1 Referring to Figure 10.1:
   a If demand increases from D_1D_1 to D_2D_2, why does the price remain constant?
   b If demand increases to D_4D_4, why will prices rise to P_y?
2 According to structuralists, which economic features prevent the expansion of output?
3 Generally speaking, why has the monetarist view of inflation been more acceptable to some economists than the structuralist view?
4 Why is a monetarist model of inflation, even when adapted, not really suitable for explaining inflation in and between LDCs?

Word study

Exercise 1A
Alternative vocabulary

Below is a list of words (and line numbers) from the text (1–17). Next to them is a list of synonyms or explanations, in mixed order (a–q). Match the words from the text with their synonyms.

1 aggregate (6)	a claim	
2 vertical (10)	b stimulating	
3 merely (12)	c repay in kind, return like for like	
4 immobilities (17)	d total	
5 disequilibria (17)	e possible	
6 chronic (18)	f upright, at right angles (90°) to the level	
7 assertion (48)	g part, aspect	
8 proxy (82)	h between, among sectors	
9 potential (88)	i not moving, fixed	
10 lagged (101)	j severe, acute	
11 fuelling (106)	k simply, only	
12 susceptibility (110)	l imbalances	
13 ultimately (116)	m deputy, substitute	
14 *inter*-sectoral (121)	n the state of being easily influenced or affected by	
15 *intra*-sectoral (121)	o delayed, from a previous period	
16 retaliate (130)	p finally, in the end	
17 facet (footnote 1)	q within, inside sectors	

Exercise 1B
Explanation

The following words are taken from the text (line numbers are given). Can you explain their meaning as used in the text? Use a dictionary if necessary.

1 budget (32)	5 recession (62)
2 liquidity (59)	6 correlation (69)
3 cycle (61)	7 deviation (88)
4 boom (61)	8 coefficient (104)

Language use

Exercise 1
Verbalising equations

Sometimes students have difficulty in talking about equations or formulae – not because of difficulty in understanding the meaning or usage, but because of uncertainty about putting the symbols into English words. Some practice is given below in verbalising the equation on page 102.

Further practice in verbalising symbols and equations is given in the Appendix 'Mathematical expressions in economics'.

Note: In the equations some of the symbols are not explained – they are:
(dot above $\dot{P}$) = proportional rate of change (i.e. growth as opposed to change)

$\quad$ P $\quad$ = price level

(superscript)^e = expectation

(subscript)$_t$ $\quad$ = time (period)

Notice how equation (1) is spoken formally:
> P dot t equals b subscript zero plus b subscript one GAP subscript t plus b subscript two P dot e t

Spoken more informally (and usually), equation (1) is
> P dot t equals b zero plus b one GAP t plus b two P dot e t

Practise reading the equations aloud. If possible practise saying them in pairs.

Exercise 2
Academic caution

In economics writing there is often the need to be **tentative** (i.e. to indicate 'less than 100 per cent certainty'). The purpose is to show that a generalisation is being made or that it is necessary to be cautious in making a statement or arriving at a conclusion. In other words, one is indicating a *high* degree of certainty, probability or possibility instead of *total* certainty.

To illustrate this feature of academic writing, some examples are shown below from units in this book (Unit and Stage numbers are given in brackets).

1 The consumer price index *may well* have a pronounced urban bias . . . (10.1)
2 Econometric testing . . . *has tended to* favour . . . (10.2)
3 Rises in import prices thus *appear to* have played an important role . . . (10.2)
4 Inflation will *almost certainly* affect the distribution of income . . . (10.2)
5 The functional distribution *may* be affected by a redistribution . . . (10.2)
6 The gains from trade *were more likely . . . to* be appropriated . . . (9.1)
7 Common sense would, therefore, *seem* to dictate . . . (8.2)
8 This is *possibly* explainable by the fact that . . . (8.2)
9 TNCs are *unlikely to* become major suppliers . . . (8.2)
10 Some combination . . . would *perhaps* make the most sense . . . (6.2)

Below is a table showing the most common ways of expressing caution or tentativeness.

through the verb	through the adverb/adjective
appear(s) (more) (likely) to	almost certainly
seem(s)	likely
tend(s) to	probably/probable
be (more) likely to	
may well	
might	maybe
may	perhaps
could	possibly/possible
can	

Note
1 Caution can also be achieved by using adverbs of frequency e.g. *usually*, *normally*, *generally*, *frequently*, *often* . . . and other qualifying adverbs e.g. *predominantly*, *mainly*, *chiefly*, *largely* . . .
2 The negative can be qualified in a similar way to remove the sense of '100 per cent negative' e.g. *is unlikely to*, *is not likely to* . . .

Open exercise
Qualify the following definite statement in *five* different ways, selected from those shown above, so that the statement becomes more cautious.
    Inflation is a problem for LDCs.

Extension activities

1 Writing: Essay
Select either your own country or one whose economy you have some knowledge of and which has suffered from inflation. You can make use of any books, articles, etc. if you wish.

Briefly describe the rate of inflation in the country in recent years. Try to explain the major causes of the inflation. What steps has the government taken to control the inflation? Has the IMF been involved in any anti-inflationary stabilisation policies?

In your writing try to use, where appropriate, some of the tentative language that was shown in Exercise 2: Academic caution.

2 Group activity: Discussion

Inflation
'The explanation of inflation has always generated controversy . . . in the context of LDCs, between monetarists and structuralists.'
The group or class should be divided into two sections. One section should represent *monetarists* and the other should represent *structuralists* – to explain the causes of inflation in LDCs. As far as possible, within each section, students should prepare their arguments in pairs, working together to note the main arguments to support their point of view (monetarist or structuralist). Reference can be made to the texts in this unit, to Table 10.1 in Stage 1, and to knowledge of the real world.

When the arguments have been prepared, one person from each side can present his/her point of view. This can be supplemented by additional arguments from other students on the same side. Questions can also be put from one side to the other in order to challenge the other side's point of view.

Answer key and notes

For the Comprehension questions, (Stage 1 open and Stage 2 post-questions), the answers given here are suggested answers; some variations are often possible. Answers are only given where they are necessary. For many of the Extension activities there is no key.

Unit 1 Stage 1

Comprehension

A1 T (evidence: lines 4–6)
  2 T (evidence: lines 20–21)
  3 F (evidence: lines 27–28)
  4 T (evidence: lines 29–31)

B1 Real income is the quantity of real goods and services that can be bought; money income is the amount of money that is received.
  2 If the rate of growth of income is greater than the rate of growth of population.
  3 GNP = GDP plus net factor (or property) incomes from abroad.
  4 Because net property income from abroad is likely to be negative.
  5 The average annual growth rate (%) was higher for all groups of countries between 1960 and 1980 than between 1950 and 1960.
  6 Middle-income countries had the same average annual growth rate as industrial countries, and a higher rate than low-income countries between 1960 and 1980.

Word study

Exercise 1A Alternative vocabulary
1 inhabitants (line 13)
2 accruing (line 14)
3 a depreciation (line 18)
4 a projection (line 27)
5 to predict (line 27)
6 to sustain (line 28)
7 a widening (line 29)
8 a gap (line 30)
Note: a widening (7 above): from the verb *to widen* = to make wide or wider
There are a number of verbs formed in the same way by adding the ending *-en* (to an adjective or noun):
e.g. to widen   to weaken
        broaden   lessen
        fatten   lengthen
        shorten   strengthen

Exercise 1B Explanation
1 any particular or specified year
2 taxes levied on goods or services rather than on individuals or companies (e.g. VAT – value added tax) (Compare – *direct tax*: a tax paid by a person or firm e.g. income tax)

Exercise 2 Economics
A1 economics   **4** economist
  2 economy   **5** economic
  3 economise   **6** economical

Exercise 3 Development
1 less developed   **3** to develop
2 developed   **4** development

Exercise 4 Rise/raise/increase
1 increased or rose
2 a rise or an increase
3 raised or increased
4 to rise or to increase
5 rises or increases; rise(s) or increase(s)

Language use

Exercise 1 Comparisons
1 lower(less) . . . than
2 lower(less) . . . than
3 as } high . . . as
    so }
4 the same (or, as high) . . . as
5 the biggest, or the largest
6 the smallest (or the lowest)

Exercise 2 Definitions
1a National income is defined as a measure of . . .
  b Elasticity is defined as a measure of . . .
2a Statistics may be defined as the branch of mathematics which is concerned with the use of . . .
  b Econometrics may be defined as the branch of economics which is concerned with the application of . . .

Unit 1 Stage 2

Comprehension

Post-questions
1 Growth without development was possible, in theory, if increases in *per capita* incomes were not accompanied either by structural changes or by the diffusion of the gains in real income among all the sectors of the population (i.e. when the benefits of growth are not distributed to all the population).
2 Only if it is explicitly assumed that all sectors in the economy grow at equal rates so as to leave the proportions of the national economy that they represent unchanged (i.e. if they grow at the same rate and their share in the GDP does not change).
3 Other indicators relate to the political, social and educational dimensions of development, and also a reduction of cultural dependence on the great powers (i.e. also self-reliance).
4 a Attempts to move GNP toward a broader welfare measure lack a logical basis and result in a confusion of concepts.

b Social indicators have not yet been produced which are readily accepted and comprehended.

c Social accounts systems have not yet overcome the difficult problems encountered.

d A composite index has not yet been produced because it has proved impossible to translate all social progress into a readily accepted common denominator.

5 The main problem is that the definitions refer to an ideal world or state of affairs (i.e. normative or utopian), and are, therefore, both ahistorical and apolitical (i.e. they are not related to the real world).

Word study

Exercise 1A Alternative vocabulary

1 d	**5** k	**9** o	**13** c
2 n	**6** a	**10** j	**14** e
3 f	**7** p	**11** b	**15** g
4 i	**8** l	**12** m	**16** h

Exercise 1B Explanation

1 Subjective assessments based on one's own code of values.

2 Standards by which something can be judged, decided or measured.

3 Here it means a general indicator; mathematically, it means the number *below* the line in a fraction that is exactly divisible by all such numbers in a group of fractions e.g. ½, ⅓, ¼ have a common denominator of 12.

Language use

Exercise 1 Relative clauses

1 In many LDCs agriculture, which is the largest sector, is very inefficient.

2 Economic growth, which is a necessary condition for economic development, is not a sufficient condition on its own to ensure an increase in economic welfare.

3 Dudley Seers, who has defined development as almost a synonym for improvement, has influenced the thinking of many economists.

4 Development can be determined by various criteria which relate to poverty, inequality, unemployment and self-reliance.

5 Hicks and Streeten, who have analysed four different approaches to the problem of measuring development, conclude that there is no viable alternative to using GNP at present.

Exercise 2 Reduced relative clauses

1 Surely the values (*that/which*) we need are staring us in the face . . . (32)

2 The search for a composite index of social welfare, (*which/that is*) analogous to GNP as an index of production . . . (69)

3 The great deal of work (*which/that has been* or *is*) devoted to composite indices . . . (72)

Exercise 3 Summary

(1) growth	(7) growth	(13) adjustments
(2) economic	(8) change	(14) accounting
(3) development	(9) normative	(15) indices
(4) GNP	(10) criteria	(16) ideal
(5) *per*	(11) indicators	(17) development
(6) *capita*	(12) self-reliance	

Unit 2 Stage 1

Comprehension

A1 F (evidence: 1–3)
2 T (evidence: 7–9)
3 F (evidence: 11–13)
4 T (evidence: 14–16)
5 T (evidence: 18–20)
6 F (evidence: 27–29)
7 F (evidence: 33–37)

B1 They serve as a good example of economic development meaning progress towards objectives which correspond to those conditions found in the advanced countries.

2 The critics said that underdevelopment was really the product of capitalist development in the metropolitan centres (or in industrialised countries).

3 They have been colonies of various metropolitan powers (e.g. UK, France etc.).

4 They became suppliers of raw materials and foodstuffs to the industrialised countries, and provided closed markets for their manufactured goods and opportunities for profitable investment.

Word study

Exercise 1A Alternative vocabulary

1 highlighted (3)
2 eliminated (8)
3 obstacles (9)
4 retarding (12)
5 prior (16)
6 associated with (31)
7 piracy (31)
8 plunder (31)

Exercise 1B Explanation

1 a continuous sequence of cause and effect; a chain of events in which response to one difficulty creates a new problem that aggravates the original difficulty

2 two aspects of the same process (i.e. the intimate links between development and underdevelopment)

3 the specialization of workers in particular parts or operations of a production process

4 areas of influence

5 markets which had no choice of alternative supplies and therefore had to buy; guaranteed markets

Exercise 2 Critic/criticise

1 critics
2 criticisms
3 critiques
4 to criticise

Exercise 3 Synonyms and antonyms

Various answers are possible.

Exercise 4 Pairs of words in economics

1 e	**8** s	**15** r	**22** q
2 h	**9** y	**16** x	**23** l
3 j	**10** z	**17** b	**24** g
4 m	**11** w	**18** u	**25** a
5 n	**12** t	**19** f	**26** d
6 p	**13** v	**20** k	
7 c	**14** i	**21** o	

Language use

Exercise 1 Verb tense: passive
1 were found
2 was argued
3 was located
4 was seen
5 was associated
6 were provided

Exercise 2 Passive: more practice
(1) were based
(2) was assumed
(3) were overcome
(4) was caused
(5) were colonised
(6) was considered
(7) was established
(8) were supplied
(9) were manufactured

Unit 2 Stage 2

Comprehension

Post-questions
1 The destruction of the old society and economy contrasted with providing the beginnings of Western society in Asia.
2 To generate a theory of dependence complementary to (additional to) the theory of imperialism.
3 By removing the LDCs' surplus and using it to generate their own development.
4 It is the process of division within LDCs whereby their advanced sectors are linked to the international capitalist system, and their backward economic sectors become 'internal colonies'.
5 The theory is static (i.e. not dynamic), and the assumptions made by some economists are doubtful (i.e. the existence of a hidden alternative to the development that actually took place – by this, Warren suggests that there was *no* superior or preferable alternative in existence).

Word study

Exercise 1A Alternative vocabulary
1 f	5 b	9 o	13 w	17 a	21 n
2 e	6 j	10 k	14 m	18 g	22 t
3 q	7 l	11 s	15 v	19 u	23 r
4 h	8 i	12 d	16 x	20 p	24 c

Exercise 1B Explanation
1 the stock of fixed capital in a country considered as a significant determinant of economic growth e.g. factories, roads, transport and communication systems, water supplies, electric power, education etc.
2 the owner-manager of a firm who, by risk and initiative, tries to make profits
3 stopped, restricted, hindered
4 collected, amassed
5 in a state of equilibrium with no changes taking place; concerned with forces that do not produce movement

Note: Compare *dynamic* – a dynamic analysis in economics is concerned with movement through time.

Exercise 2 Negative prefixes (1)
A1
unacceptable	unemployment	unprofitable
uncertain	unequal	unsatisfactory
unchanged	unimportant	unstable
undeveloped	unnecessary	unsuccessful
uneconomic	unorthodox	

2
inaccurate	indirect	informally
indefinite	indistinct	insignificant
independent	inefficient	insufficient

B
logical	illogical
literate	illiterate
legible	illegible
legitimate	illegitimate
legal	illegal

possibility	impossibility
balance	imbalance
permanent	impermanent
moral	immoral
precise	imprecise
patient	impatient
personal	impersonal
mature	immature
perfect	imperfect
mobility	immobility

religious	irreligious
responsible	irresponsible
regular	irregular
relevant	irrelevant
replaceable	irreplaceable

Exercise 3 Negative prefixes (2)
1 Projections of economic growth are generally *inaccurate*.
2 In many ways, using GNP *per capita* as an indicator of economic welfare is *unsatisfactory*.
3 The *immobility* of labour is a factor to consider in economic development.
4 Initially, development economics was an *indistinct* area of study.
5 Some of the early theories of economic development are *irrelevant* today.

Exercise 4 Formation of adjectives
1
structural	managerial
cultural	entrepreneurial
historical	peripheral
mystical	theoretical

2
colony	influence
industry	society
nation	politics

Language use

Exercise 1 Reference skills (1)
1 T	5 P	9 D	13 E	17 S
2 J	6 B	10 K	14 F	18 H
3 A	7 C	11 L	15 G	19 O
4 R	8 M	12 Q	16 N	20 I

Exercise 2 Reference skills (2)
1 J, T, N, S
2 B, C, D, F, K, L, R, T
3 B, C, D, M, P, R, S

Exercise 3 Summary
(1) Karl
(2) Marx
(3) colonialism
(4) framework
(5) neo-Marxism
(6) Paul
(7) Baran
(8) surplus
(9) underdeveloped
(10) dependent
(11) sectors
(12) dependency
(13) Warren
(14) critic
(15) static
(16) forms
(17) LDCs

Extension activities

1 Writing: Essay – notes
The introductory paragraph for this essay (which is based upon the Stage 2 text) could include the following:
1 The essay will begin by defining the central problem (*viz.* by explaining the growth and development expectations of LDCs, in particular where they have differed from the expectations expressed by Marx).
2 After this will follow an explanation of the emergence of neo-Marxism, and the relationship between neo-Marxism and dependency theories.
3 Finally, there will be a critique of neo-Marxism by Warren.

2 Pairwork: notes
1 Examples of possible questions on the writers are:
  1 What did Karl Marx emphasize in his writings of the impact of British rule on India?
  2 Has Warren's argument been accepted as the new general theory of underdevelopment?
  3 How did Warren criticise dependency theory?
  4 What is Baran's view of capital accumulation in LDCs?
  5 How did Frank extend Baran's work?
2 Some examples of suitable openings for questions are:
  Who said the following . . .?
  Where is this quotation from . . .?
  Where did this quotation come from . . .?
  When did X say this . . .?
  Which writer said . . .?

Unit 3   Stage 1

Comprehension

A1 T   **4** T
  2 T   **5** T
  3 F

B1 The 'special case' was the private-enterprise, developed industrial economy . . .
  2 Because propositions obtained from mainly static analysis were irrelevant and perhaps misleading and that not enough attention had been given to the particular political and institutional structures of the LDCs.
  3 The LDCs' position was determined by the 'openness' of their economies, their dependence on the developed industrial economies as markets for their mainly primary product exports and their vulnerability to protective measures imposed by such economies.
  4 No, it was not appropriate.

Word study

Exercise 1A   Alternative vocabulary
1 initiated (3)	**8** subject to (23)
2 formidable (8)	**9** biases (24)
3 exogenous (8)	**10** parameters (25)
4 conceded (10)	**11** variables (26)
5 derived (13)	**12** assign (31)
6 divorced from (16)	**13** presuppose (35)
7 vulnerability to (19)	

Note the differences between the following words:
indigenous (from 2.2) = originating in a country or region; native to; internal
exogenous = originating from the outside due to external causes
endogenous = growing from within; determined within the system
e.g. *Indigenous* entrepreneurs find it difficult to compete with transnational corporations.
The LDC is subject to a variety of powerful *exogenous* shocks.
For the structuralist economist, the money supply is an *endogenous* variable.

Exercise 1B   Explanation
1 An economy which engages in international trade; the degree of openness of an economy may be approximated by the size of the ratio of exports and imports to National Income.
Note: a closed economy: a concept used mainly in theoretical models to describe an economy with no external trade (which is completely self-sufficient and insulated from external forces).
2 Raw materials (i.e. unmanufactured) from natural resources e.g. from mining, agriculture, fishing, forestry.
3 The sum total of separate units when collected together.

Exercise 2   Past tense forms
1a denied		**d** implied	
b allied		**e** replied	
c identified		**f** studied	

Note: This formation occurs if the letter before *-y* is a **consonant** letter. If it is a **vowel** letter (a, e, i, o, u) there are different changes e.g. *play – played, stay – stayed*; but *lay – laid, say – said*

2 verb infinitive	past simple tense	past participle
a break	broke	broken
b bring	brought	brought
c find	found	found
d give	gave	given
e hide	hid	hidden
f lead	led	led
g leave	left	left
h make	made	made
i mean	meant	meant
j overcome	overcame	overcome
k pay	paid	paid
l see	saw	seen
m take	took	taken
n underlie	underlay	underlain

Language use

Exercise 1   Prepositions
(1) For	(10) in, within	(19) of
(2) over, about	(11) of	(20) within, in
(3) of	(12) of	(21) of
(4) to	(13) of	(22) on, upon
(5) by	(14) to	(23) for
(6) in	(15) of, in	(24) to
(7) with, by	(16) In	(25) by
(8) of	(17) of	
(9) of	(18) from	

Unit 3 Stage 2

Comprehension

Post-questions

1 Streeten's main criticism was that a number of the models do not have the essential components i.e. they should be realistic, relevant and useful.
2 Little's view is that the price mechanism is the best mechanism and that it should work well.
3 The success that a number of LDCs have had recently in entering export markets for manufactured goods; also if factor prices are 'right', firms will substitute cheaper labour for more expensive capital.
4 Generally, orthodox Keynesian macro-economic theory was thought not to be relevant for LDCs. Certainly this was so for short- and medium-term macro-economic management in LDCs.
5 It should help to encourage greater communication between the various development specialists and result in a more complete understanding of the problems of poverty and inequality, and in policy prescriptions that can be made more relevant and realistic.

Word study

Exercise 1A Alternative vocabulary

1 l	6 s	11 a	16 b
2 m	7 o	12 k	17 p
3 e	8 g	13 r	18 n
4 f	9 q	14 j	19 c
5 i	10 h	15 d	

Exercise 1B Explanation

1 practical evidence; data or proof from observation and experience
2 equilibrium price (the true marginal value of a good or opportunity cost of a resource, and which may differ from the market price)
3 those methods of production that use proportionately more labour than the other factors of production e.g. hand-made goods, service industries. A *capital-intensive* process of production is one which uses proportionately more capital relative to the quantities of other inputs.

Language use

Exercise 1 Verb tense: present simple

(1) argues		(7) support	
(2) distrust		(8) encourage	
(3) seek		(9) point out	
(4) view		(10) exists	
(5) believe		(11) gives	
(6) works			

Exercise 2 Negatives

1 (1) neither   (5) no
  (2) nor   (6) not
  (3) not only   (7) do/did not
  (4) but also

2a If a model did not have relevance, then it was not useful.
 b If a model had no relevance, then it was not useful.
 c Unless a model had relevance, it was not useful.
 d If a model lacked relevance, then it was not useful.

3 The following are suggested answers; a number of variations are possible.
 a LDCs are often not only *poor* but also *over-populated*.
 b In many cases, LDCs have neither *wealth* nor *a developed infrastructure*.
 c When discussing the causes of inflation there is often no *agreement among economists*.
 d Unless a theory *is relevant, it will not be useful*.

Exercise 3 Summary: missing words

Missing words are shown in italics next to the relevant line number.

1 conventional *economic* theory
2 and *Bauer*, resisted
3 best *mechanism* for
4 even *in* LDCs.
5 neo-classical *economist*, tried
6 between *structuralist* and
7 be *inflexible*: they
8 the *price* mechanism
9 The *neo-classical* supporters
10 in *support* of
11 a *number* of
12 neo-classical *school* has
13 the *techniques* of
14 that *projects* are
15 have *criticised/attacked* both
16 the *methods/methodology* used
17 little *discussion* of
18 to *LDCs*. However
19 is *beginning* to
20 particular *structural* features
21 an *advance*, it
22 multi-disciplinary *development* studies.
23 would *lead* to
24 and *inequality* at

Unit 4 Stage 1

Comprehension

A1 T 2 F 3 T 4 F 5 T

B1 Yes.
2 Because of the restricted availability to them of productive assets (particularly agricultural land).
3 A nutritional norm involves specifying quantities of calories and proteins. These will differ according to a number of factors e.g. age, sex, climate, type of work undertaken. There are also complex relationships between nutrition, health, education and fertility.
4 Because there is no one absolute biological standard to cover all people throughout the world. Poverty levels will always vary with the general level of economic, social and political development. Therefore, there will always be an arbitrary element in the definition of absolute poverty. ('Poverty' in one country may not be 'poverty' in another country.)

Word study

Exercise 1A Alternative vocabulary

1 e	3 g	5 c	7 b	9 d	11 a
2 j	4 k	6 h	8 f	10 i	

Exercise 1B   Explanation

1 All the people living in one house i.e. family, lodgers, etc.
2 That part of Africa south of the Sahara desert (e.g. countries such as Chad, Niger, Nigeria, etc., it excludes the countries in the north *viz*. Algeria, Egypt, Libya, Morocco etc.).
3 There are relatively too many poor people living in the country areas; or: The number of poor (people) living in rural areas is out of all proportion; or: There is a big disparity in the number of poor (people) living in the rural areas (compared with those living in the urban areas).
4 Anything owned by an individual or a firm and which has a money value; *productive or fixed assets* are, for example, land, buildings, plant, machinery, vehicles; current assets are e.g., cash, bank deposits etc. *Note:* the opposite is '*liabilities*'.
5 The necessary consumption or inputs.

Exercise 2   Continents, regions, countries and currencies

1 Africa, Asia, Europe, North America, South America
2 SCANDINAVIA
Denmark, Iceland, Norway, Sweden

THE MIDDLE EAST
Egypt, Iran, Iraq, Saudi Arabia

THE FAR EAST
China, Japan, North Korea, South Korea

SOUTHEAST ASIA
Burma, Indonesia, Malaysia, Thailand

LATIN AMERICA
Argentina, Brazil, Mexico, Peru

SUB-SAHARAN AFRICA
Chad, Mali, Niger, Sudan

3

country	adjective	currency
Brazil	Brazilian	cruzeiro
China	Chinese	yuan
Denmark	Danish	krone
Egypt	Egyptian	pound
France	French	franc
Germany	German	mark
Greece	Greek	drachma
Hong Kong	Hong Kong	dollar
India	Indian	rupee
Iran	Iranian	rial
Italy	Italian	lira
Japan	Japanese	yen
Kenya	Kenyan	shilling
Malaysia	Malaysian	ringgit
Mexico	Mexican	peso
Netherlands (Holland)	Dutch	guilder
Nigeria	Nigerian	naira
Portugal	Portuguese	escudo
Saudi Arabia	Saudi Arabian	riyal
Spain	Spanish	peseta
Sweden	Swedish	krona
Thailand	Thai	baht
UK | England | Britain	English | British	| pound sterling
USA	American	dollar
USSR	Russian	rouble
Venezuela	Venezuelan	bolivar

Language use

Exercise 1   Plurality; fractions

1 Open
2a $\frac{1}{2}$, $\frac{1}{6}$, $\frac{1}{3}$
  b a/one quarter, two-thirds, three-quarters, five-sixths, seven-eighths, nine-tenths.

Unit 4   Stage 2

Comprehension

Post-questions

1 Yes, they are often taken as indicators of the extent of inequality in general.
2 Diagram 3.
3 Data on the size distribution of income from different countries have been used by a number of economists to suggest that there is a link. However, little evidence exists regarding the relationship between economic growth and the functional distribution of income.
4 Savings, capital accumulation, patterns of consumption (or composition of imports and output of domestic manufacturing sector . . .).
5 Yes. Governments have often found the variety of policy instruments inadequate, or ineffective – mainly because of the 'vested interests' of groups of influential people.
6 Yes – at least in the immediate future.

Word study

Exercise 1A   Alternative vocabulary

1	e	**6**	m	**11**	a	**15**	q
2	g	**7**	h	**12**	p	**16**	b
3	r	**8**	c	**13**	n	**17**	o
4	j	**9**	l	**14**	i	**18**	d
5	k	**10**	f				

Exercise 1B   Explanation

1 in the second (i.e. LDCs) than in the first (i.e. developed countries)
2 giving up one thing in return for another
3 one of the factors, that influences or affects; partly determine

Language use

Exercise 1   Other, others, another

(1) On the other hand   (3) Other
(2) another   (4) others

Extension activities

2 Pyramid discussion

There is a deliberate overlap among a number of the choices in order to allow for discussion among the students about what is included or excluded, and whether some items can be subsumed by others. Different interpretations are possible with some of the choices – a student may look at them from the point of view of an individual or from the point of view of the country as a whole. In the discussion students can clarify what they mean by an item.

Unit 5 Stage 1

Comprehension

A1 F (It should be the *percentage* of the total
population)
  2 T
  3 F (It was 4 per cent until *1980*, thereafter some
decline until 2000.)
  4 F (It should be 40 cities in the *less developed* world.)
  5 F (There are differences in urbanisation patterns but
similarities in problems.)

B1 More and more people are living in towns and cities.
It is likely that more than half the world's population
will be living in urban areas by the year 2000.
  2 There will be more very large cities in LDCs than in
developed countries : 40 cities of 5 million or more
people in LDCs compared with 12 in developed
countries.
  3 The advantages are the creation of new opportunities
for increases in productivity and incomes, and
decreases in poverty. The disadvantages are the
problems associated with providing: urban
employment opportunities; urban transport facilities;
adequate housing, health and educational facilities.
There are also problems of overcrowding and
pollution.

Word study

Exercise 1A Alternative vocabulary
1 c   **2** f   **3** a   **4** e   **5** d   **6** b

Exercise 1B Explanation
1,000,000,000 (a thousand million) – this is the USA
system which is generally replacing the old British system
of 1,000,000,000,000 (a million million).

Language use

Exercise 1 Prepositions with dates and figures
(1) Between	(8) by	(15) In	(21) In
(2) of	(9) by/in	(16) at	(22) in
(3) in	(10) of	(17) of	(23) of
(4) from	(11) in	(18) for/in/	(24) By/In
(5) to	(12) of	during	(25) of
(6) in/during	(13) at	(19) from	(26) with/to
(7) of	(14) in/within	(20) to	(27) in

Exercise 2 Information transfer – a graph
*Figure 5.1: Proportion of the world's population living in
towns and cities* or: *Percentage of total population of the
world living in urban areas*

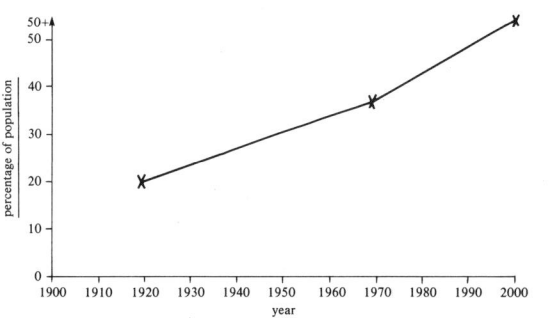

Unit 5 Stage 2

Comprehension

Post-questions

1 According to Streeten the concept of 'employment'
assumes a fairly uniform mobile labour force which
wants to work, and is able to, and can be motivated. In
LDCs a 'labour force' may not satisfy these
requirements.
2 The workers' lack of access to land, capital, and other
productive factors and education and health facilities,
combined with social and cultural attitudes and
institutional structures.
3 Where there were no unemployment benefits, there
were still low levels of unemployment. This meant that
people were finding some kind of work. Therefore it
was necessary to look more closely at the kind of work
that they did. It was found to be in small-scale
activities in the urban informal sector.
4 Ease of entry into the activity, reliance on local
resources, labour-intensive, small-scale operations,
family ownership, skills obtained outside the formal
educational system, and unregulated and competitive
markets.
5 No – there are more basic issues to be resolved first.
These relate to which development strategies are
chosen, and which development objectives are
followed.

Word study

Exercise 1A Alternative vocabulary
1 e	**5** g	**9** b	**13** c	**17** a
2 k	**6** r	**10** l	**14** p	**18** d
3 q	**7** n	**11** s	**15** f	**19** o
4 i	**8** m	**12** j	**16** h	

Exercise 1B Explanation
1 workers who may be working full-time but producing
very little (i.e. with low or zero marginal productivity)
('disguised' = concealed, hidden)
2 conversion back into a useful product e.g. especially
waste paper, glass, etc.

Language use

Exercise 1 Although and but
1 Although Frank's ideas have been extremely
influential, they have been increasingly criticised.
2 Although Seers conceded that certain elementary
propositions retained their general validity in the
context of LDCs, he was particularly critical of the
application of macro-economic concepts and models.
3 Although inequality is low in a traditional society, it
rises as economic growth accelerates.
4 Seers, Streeten and other like-minded economists
mounted a powerful and sustained onslaught on
orthodox economics, but the established orthodoxy
was by no means defeated.
5 In principle a variety of policy instruments exist to
assist the achievement of distributional objectives, but
in practice they are often inadequate or ineffective.
6 Some decline in the rate of growth of urban population
is expected for the remainder of this century, but the
urban areas of the LDCs will still have to absorb an
additional one billion people by the year 2000.

Exercise 2 Information transfer – a pie chart/diagram

Figure 5.2: Employment in LDCs in 1977

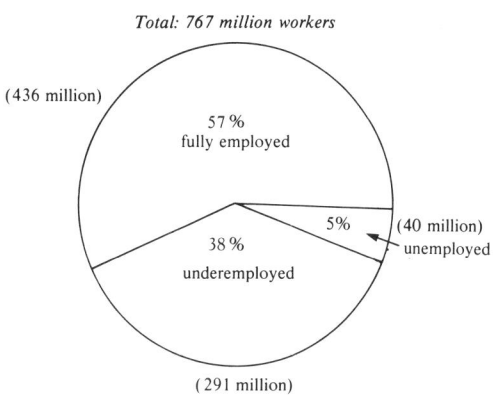

Total: 767 million workers

(436 million)

57 %
fully employed

5% (40 million)
unemployed

38 %
underemployed

(291 million)

Unit 6 Stage 1

Comprehension

A1 T
  2 F – *at least* not *only* a quarter (25 per cent)
  3 T
  4 F
  5 F

B1 No. The long-term aim of LDCs (by the year 2000) is to account for at least 25 per cent of world manufacturing value added.
  2 The rate of growth was slower for LDCs with the lowest and highest incomes. For the upper-middle income countries there was a slight increase in the growth rate – to 8.5 per cent p.a. (1970–1978) compared to 7.7 per cent p.a. in the earlier period.
  3 The upper-middle income countries grew the fastest between 1960 and 1970 and their growth rate was 7.7 per cent p.a.
  4 Basically uneven. There has been increasing differentiation between different LDCs. Relatively few countries have experienced rapid and sustained industrialisation. Many LDCs have not yet experienced industrial development and structural change.

Word study

Exercise 1A Alternative vocabulary
1 d   **2** f   **3** e   **4** b*   **5** a   **6** c

*Note: implying that, although other people use this description, label, or term, the writer might not use it himself.

Exercise 1B Explanation
Prices are held constant (fixed) with respect to a given base year i.e. we measure the growth of the physical volume of output.

Exercise 2 Industry, industrialise, manufacture
1 (1) industrialist (possibly, manufacturer)
  (2) industrial
2 (3) manufacturer (possibly, industrialist)
  (4) manufacturing (possibly, manufactured)

3 (5) industrialisation
  (6) industries (possibly, manufacturing industries)
4 (7) Industrial
  (8) industry (possibly, industries)
  (9) manufacture
  (10) industrialised (or, industrial)

Language use

Exercise 1 Information transfer – a histogram or bar chart
Note: This is also called a *bar graph.*

Figure 6.1: Average percentage growth per annum of manufacturing value added in LDCs

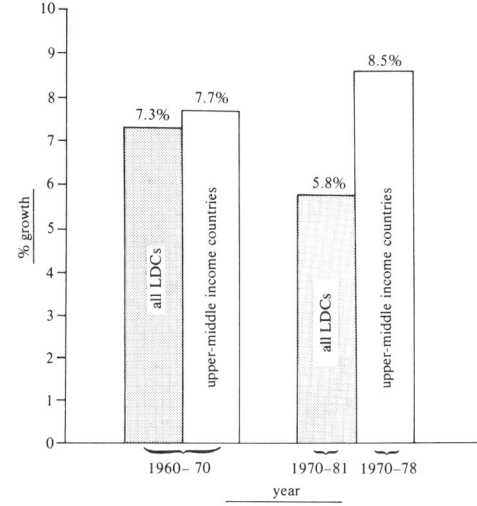

7.3%   7.7%

8.5%

5.8%

all LDCs

upper-middle income countries

all LDCs

upper-middle income countries

% growth

10
9
8
7
6
5
4
3
2
1
0

1960– 70   1970–81   1970–78

year

Unit 6 Stage 2

Comprehension

Post-questions

1 Large-scale, capital-intensive, urban-based industries, existing largely for the needs of middle- and upper-income groups.
2 They argue that industrialisation has now become part of the problem itself. ISI has created a dependent industrial structure, dominated by foreign capital and technology and without a machine-making sector.
3 Very important. For example, between 1960 and 1977 the average real growth rate of manufactured exports from LDCs was 12.3 per cent p.a. The share of manufactured goods in total merchandise exports (excluding oil) rose from 25.4 per cent in 1965 to 45.1 per cent in 1976.
4 The NICs have been successful and have had high rates of growth of output and employment but the export-led strategy of industrialisation has had problems. The export growth of NICs is very dependent on the state of the economies of the developed countries which take about two-thirds of their manufactured exports. The NICs are very vulnerable to protectionism in those economies. There are other problems – balance of payments difficulties, poverty and unemployment still continue; and there may continue to be a dependence on foreign capital and technology.

5 The structuralist solutions include: the regulation of TNCs, the development of a domestic capital goods sector (with indigenous technological development), and the establishment of mass markets for the output of domestic industries.

Word study

Exercise 1A Alternative vocabulary

1 j	6 r	11 a	16 m
2 c	7 n	12 g	17 d*
3 f	8 t	13 q	18 k
4 h	9 s	14 b	19 i
5 l	10 p	15 o	20 e

*Note: Do not confuse the verb *adopt* with the verb *adapt*.

Exercise 1B Explanation

1 A tariff is a tax levied by a government on imports (for the purposes of protection, support of the balance of payments, or the raising of revenue). Tariff barriers are taxes imposed at a high level in order to restrict, prevent or discourage imports.

2 A monopoly exists when a firm produces and sells the entire output of some commodity (or, in practice, a large proportion of the output): 'monopolistic' is the adjective from the noun 'monopoly'.

3 The terms of trade normally relate to the international situation and refer to the ratio of the index of export prices to the index of import prices. An improvement in the terms of trade follows if export prices rise more quickly than import prices (or fall more slowly than import prices). Here, the domestic terms of trade refer to the relationship within the country between the agricultural sector and the industrial sector, i.e. the ratio of index of prices of agricultural goods to index of prices of manufactured goods.

4 A financial statement of the difference over a given period between total payments to foreign nations, arising from imports of goods and services and transfers abroad of capital, interest, grants, etc., and total receipts from foreign nations, arising from the exports of goods and services and transfers from abroad of capital, interest, grants, etc.

Language use

Exercise 1 Cause and effect

1a has permitted	c have contributed to
b has led to	d may well induce

e *As a result of* this trend, there has been a significant change in the composition of LDC exports.
(CAUSE / EFFECT)

Note: For more information and practice in cause and effect see *Academic Writing Course*, R. R. Jordan (1980), Collins. Unit 6: Cause and effect.

Exercise 2 Should: prescription

1 TNCs should be regulated
2 a domestic capital goods sector should be developed
3 indigenous technological development should be encouraged
4 mass markets for the output of domestic industries should be created
5 income and assets should be redistributed
6 government expenditure should be increased

Unit 7 Stage 1

Comprehension

A1 F   **2** T   **3** F   **4** T   **5** F

B1 Factories, mines, sales offices
2 The possession of a minimum number of affiliates, or operation in a minimum number of host countries.

3 *Transnational corporations*

criteria TNCs	... with min. of 1 foreign affiliate	... in 2 or more host countries	... in 6 or more host countries
Number of TNCs in 1977	10,373	5,586	2,050
US TNCs % of total TNCs	26.8%	—	36.9%

4 Various measures of foreign content (e.g. exports, sales, assets, earnings or employment); also criteria relating to organisational form, motivation and the structure of decision-making or control in the TNC.

Word study

Exercise 1A Alternative vocabulary

1 c	4 f	6 d
2 a	5 g	7 b
3 e		

Exercise 1B Explanation

Generally, 'host countries' means countries which provide facilities, but here it means countries in which direct foreign investment (DFI) is located or where a TNC otherwise conducts operations.

Language use

Exercise 1 More definitions

1a a firm	d an enterprise
b a company	e a corporation
c an affiliate	f an industry

2 The following are suggestions; other definitions are possible.
  a *An asset* is any item of value which is owned and which may be useful to meet debts.
  b *A business* is an individual or group of individuals who are engaged in a trade, service or commercial activity with a view to making a profit.
  c *A factory* is a building which is normally equipped with machinery where workers are employed in the manufacture of goods.

Exercise 2 Exemplification

The following are examples of answers; in some cases alternatives are possible.
1 For example, TNCs from the USA ... (Stage 1, 10)
2 e.g., the possession of a minimum number of affiliates ..., (Stage 1, 5)
3 (countries such as the Bahamas ...) (Stage 2, 14)
4 (exports, sales, assets, earnings or employment) ... (Stage 1, 17)

5 – factories, mines, sales offices and the like – (Stage 1, 2)
6 In 1977, there were 5,586 firms . . . in six or more host countries. (Stage 1, 7)
7 Examples of such ownership-specific advantages are marketing skills, . . . (Stage 2, 37)
8 Such strategies include heavy reliance . . . (Stage 2, 74)

Exercise 3   Back reference
1 a TNC (1)
2 the possession of a minimum number of affiliates or operation in a minimum number of host countries (e.g. in 2 or more, or 6 or more, host countries) (5)
3 TNCs from the USA account for 26.8 per cent . . . but for 36.9 per cent of all firms which operate in 6 or more host countries. (11)
4 US TNCs (15)

Unit 7   Stage 2

Comprehension

Post-questions
1 Because direct foreign investment by the TNCs provides, in 'package' form, those resources otherwise not available to LDCs (e.g. technology, marketing skills), or only available in insufficient quantities (e.g. capital, enterprise).
2 The group of 10 countries (semi-industrialised economies) together with the OPEC countries and tax havens.
3 Access to raw materials, utilisation of cheap labour, and supplying host country markets (and maximisation of global profits).
4 DFI (by internalising their assets).
5 Through product differentiation, advertising, rapid technological innovation of both products and processes and through competitive entry to LDC markets.
6 They include heavy reliance on the re-investment of profits and local borrowing to finance affiliate operations, the take-over of existing firms, and the manipulation of transfer prices (in order to avoid tax payments, to by-pass exchange control regulations or to minimise liabilities in weak currencies).

Word study

Exercise 1A   Alternative vocabulary

1 e*	4 t	7 r	10 s	13 y	16 c	19 q	22 u
2 f	5 h	8 j	11 l	14 p	17 x	20 w	23 m
3 k	6 o	9 v	12 a	15 n	18 i	21 b	24 g
							25 d

*Note: the plural is *phenomena*

Exercise 1B   Explanation
1 The sectors concerned with mining, removing or separating minerals or metals.
2 The creation of real or imagined differences in essentially the same type of product, by means of branding, packaging, advertising etc. It is most common in consumer goods industries e.g. washing powders, cars, cigarettes. The purpose of product differentiation is to build up 'consumer loyalty' to one firm's product or brand.

3 A market situation in which each of a few producers affects the market without any one of them having decisive control over it.
4 Also known as 'soft currencies'. A currency whose exchange rate tends to fall because of persistent balance of payments deficits. Governments are unwilling to hold a soft or weak currency in their foreign exchange reserves as it is not easily convertible. The opposite expression is 'hard currency' or 'strong' or 'scarce' currency.
5 A name or distinctive symbol put on goods produced by a particular firm and reserved exclusively for use by that firm.

Language use

Exercise 1   Sequence: summary
1 *Figure 7.1   TNC investment in LDCs (DFI)*

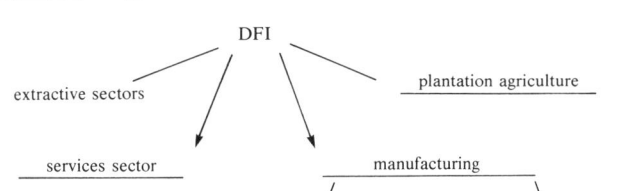

2
1 c	5 g	9 k	
2 f	6 b	10 a	
3 h	7 i	11 e	
4 j	8 d		

3 Several variations are possible; the following is a suggestion.
TNCs invest in LDCs for a number of reasons. *But* why should DFI be used instead of other arrangements? If DFI is to be profitable, the TNC must possess ownership-specific advantages. *It is argued that* the TNC can most profitably exploit these advantages through DFI. It is *thus* by internalising its assets that the TNC can profit most from its special advantages. We must *also* take into account (, however,) location-specific factors. *Three further points are: firstly*, TNCs dominate in oligopolistic market structures. *Secondly*, TNCs organise their operations on a world-wide scale. *Thirdly, it can be assumed that* the maximisation of world-wide profits is the long-term aim. *It should be noted that* DFI can be important in a number of LDCs, even if the TNC is small. *Finally, it should also be noted* that non-equity operations have become increasingly important to TNCs.

Unit 8   Stage 1

Comprehension

A1 F		3 F		5 T	
2 F		4 F		6 T	

B1 By process technology we mean how something is made, whereas product technology involves the nature and specification of what is made.

2 LDCs can acquire the managerial skills etc. either through DFI or through the various non-equity arrangements.

3 Proprietary technology is technical or commercial information which is kept secret by those that own or control it.

4 If an LDC decides to buy technology it needs to ask a further question – is it best to acquire the technology as part of the DFI package, or is it preferable to obtain the technology through some other channel?

5 LDCs would hope to make better use of imported technologies and generate new technologies themselves.

Word study

Exercise 1A Alternative vocabulary
1 d	**3** b	**5** a	
2 e	**4** f	**6** c	

Exercise 1B Explanation
1 The stock of goods which are used in production and which have themselves been produced (they are non-consumable goods).

2 Goods which are used in the production of other goods, rather than for final consumption e.g. steel (i.e. they are not finished goods).

Language use

Exercise 1 Questions forms
1 What does technology include?   or
Does technology include both process technology and product technology?   or
(What processes are included in the concept of technology?)

2 Is technology an essential input to production?   or
(What is technology an essential input to?)

3 Can technology be acquired by LDCs (in a variety of forms)?   or
(How can technology be acquired by LDCs?)

4 Are capital goods bought and sold in markets?   or
Where are capital goods bought and sold?

5 Does human labour have the capacity to make use of the equipment and techniques available?   or
Has human labour the capacity . . . etc.?   or
(What does human labour have the capacity to do?)   or
(Who has the capacity to make use . . . etc.?)

6 Is some/any information provided in markets?   or
Where is some information provided?   or
What is provided in markets?

7 Does the acquisition of technology pose a number of important problems for LDCs?   or
What does the acquisition of technology pose for LDCs?   or
What are the consequences of the acquisition of technology for LDCs?

8 Can definite answers at present be given to these questions?   or
(When can definitive answers be given to these questions?)

Exercise 2 Questions: further practice
1 What does technology include (in addition to process and product technology)?   or:
What does a definition of technology include?

2 How can LDCs obtain financial and marketing skills etc.?

3 Where are the various non-equity arrangements referred to?

4 Is proprietary technology provided in markets?   or
Is proprietary technology freely available?

5 Is there an increased awareness of the issues involved?   or
Is the increased awareness of the issues involved having an effect?

Unit 8 Stage 2

Comprehension

Post-questions
1 An isoquant is an equal output line/curve which shows all combinations of the two inputs (capital and labour) which can be used to produce any given level of output.

2 The point of tangency (u) is where the isoquant and isocost lines touch and where output will be maximised, given the cost constraint.

3 Neo-classical critics argue that in LDCs market prices do not reflect social opportunity costs. They say that labour is too expensive and capital is too cheap and therefore 'cheap' capital will be substituted for 'expensive' labour. They also argue that firms have less need to reduce costs and become more efficient because there is a lack of strong competition in LDCs.
  Structuralist critics have argued that there is only a limited possibility of substituting factors in the production process.

4 The evidence is ambiguous and incomplete, that is, it is not clear and sufficiently conclusive to be able to answer questions about choice of production techniques.

5 No systematic and consistent differences regarding choice of production techniques are found between matched pairs of TNCs and local firms. The conclusion regarding TNCs is that they are unlikely to become major suppliers of 'appropriate' product or process technologies to LDCs. In addition, the TNC is unlikely to have ownership-specific advantages regarding the development of such processes or products.

Word study

Exercise 1A Alternative vocabulary
1 p	**3** h	**5** o	**7** l	**9** a	**11** n	**13** m	**15** b
2 e	**4** g	**6** i	**8** c	**10** k	**12** d	**14** j	**16** f

Exercise 1B Explanation
1 Also known as 'inputs'. Traditionally, they are grouped into land, labour and capital. They are the resources needed to produce a commodity.

2 The relationship between two amounts, determined by the number of times one contains the other e.g. the ratio of 10 to 5 is 2 to 1 (often written as 2:1).

3 The point on a curve where the line touches.

4 The total expenditure in an economy on goods and

services which are used up within a specified period of time (generally a year). This expenditure includes consumer goods and services, and also raw materials used in the production processes. (A consumer is a person who purchases goods and services for his or her own personal needs. The opposite is 'producer'.)

Language use

Exercise 1 Describing a diagram
1 Choice of techniques of production for LDCs
   or: Isoquant and isocost lines
   (Others may be possible)
2 (1) capital
   (2) (the price of) labour
   (3) output (Y)
   Note: the symbol ' is said 'prime': thus u' is said 'u prime'.
   (4) u'
   (5) k'
   (6) l' amount of labour
   (7) more expensive labour
   (8) capital-intensive
   (9) lower level

Note: 'The price of labour is *too* high.' } (lines 33–35)
'The price of capital is *too* low.'

Too indicates excess. Notice the difference in meaning between *too* and *very* e.g.
Some economic theory is *very* difficult to understand.
   (But I *can* understand it.)
Some economic theory is *too* difficult to understand.
   (So I *cannot* understand it.)

Extension activities

1 Writing: Essay
When you are giving your own point of view it can be introduced by a phrase such as *In my opinion* or *From my point of view*.

2 Group activity: Pyramid discussion
Open – but bear in mind that some products are produced by more labour-intensive methods of production than others (which are produced by more capital-intensive techniques). Remember also that sometimes there may be only one way of producing a particular product.

Unit 9 Stage 1

Comprehension

A1 F   **3** T   **5** T
2 T   **4** T   **6** F

B1 Coffee represents 90 per cent of Burundi's exports; coffee represents 50 per cent of Colombia's exports; copper represents 70 per cent of Zambia's exports; etc.
2 Some critics said that any gains to LDCs from trade were likely to be taken by the developed countries. Some neo-Marxist critics said that trade was actually a disadvantage to LDCs, causing underdevelopment and poverty.
3 It is the ratio of the unit price of exports to the unit price of imports $\left(\frac{Px}{Pm}\right)$.

Word study

Exercise 1A Alternative vocabulary
1 c   **4** e   **7** a
2 h   **5** g   **8** b
3 f   **6** i   **9** d

Exercise 1B Explanation
1 Consumer goods, like washing machines, cars and TV sets, which yield services or utility over time, rather than being completely used up at the moment of consumption. Often the goods referred to are relatively expensive and technologically sophisticated.
2 A hypothesis is a theoretical proposition (which may be right or wrong) about any set of phenomena and which is capable of being tested against facts.
   Note: the plural of hypothesis is hypothes*es*.

Unit 9 Stage 2

Comprehension

Post-questions
1 Yes, there was an increase in the rate of growth of export volume in the 1970s (7.6 per cent p.a.) compared with the 1960s (5.1 per cent p.a.). However, there was a fall in the purchasing power of exports (from 5.7 per cent p.a. down to 4.5 per cent p.a.) because of the worsening terms of trade (from 0.6 down to −2.9 per cent p.a.).
2 Throughout the period 1950 to 1980 the share of least-developed LDCs in world exports continued to fall (from 1.5 per cent to 0.3 per cent). The share of all LDCs declined between 1950 and 1972 (from 30.8 per cent to 17.8 per cent) but then increased from 1973 to 1980 (up to 28.1 per cent).
3 The trends in the shares of food and fuels in LDC exports were almost exactly the opposite to each other. The share of food more than halved (from 36.5 per cent in 1955 to 16.4 per cent in 1978), while the share of fuels more than doubled (from 25.2 per cent to 52.8 per cent).
4 The value of exports in the period increased more than the value of imports, thus reducing the deficit in the trade balance (from −$19.3 billion to −$6.1 billion). There was also a reduction in the current account deficits.
5 Large, medium- and long-term debts were accrued during the 1970s, but the resources needed to service the debts also grew rapidly. The total amount of long-term external debt increased significantly. This meant that LDCs would have to maintain a high level of exports in order to service the debts. If exports declined, there would be difficulties.
6 Although trade has been a dynamic element for many LDCs (especially the major oil exporters and the NICs), some LDCs have not benefited fully e.g. sub-Saharan Africa (they need to greatly improve their structures of production and trade).

Word study

Exercise 1A Alternative vocabulary
1 d   **4** m   **7** a   **10** l   **13** e
2 h   **5** k   **8** o   **11** c   **14** b
3 j   **6** i   **9** n   **12** f   **15** g

Exercise 1B Explanation

1 The time after the war. If no war is specified, as here, it usually refers to the Second World War i.e. 1939–1945.
2 Material for producing heat or other forms of energy e.g. wood, coal, oil, gas etc.
3 To meet interest and capital payments on debts.

Language use

Exercise 1 Commenting on data (tables)

1 *Table 9.1:* For the fast-growing exporters of manufactures, the annual average rate of growth of exports was 5.8 per cent for the period 1960–70 and 11.8 per cent for the period 1970–80. The purchasing power of their exports rose by 7.0 per cent *per annum* and 8.2 per cent *per annum* respectively during the two decades. For the least developed LDCs, on the other hand, the annual average rate of growth of exports was considerably lower during these two periods (4.4 per cent and −0.4 per cent) and their purchasing power of exports actually fell by −2.2 per cent in the latter period.

2 *Table 9.2:*
a In 1950, the major oil exporters accounted for only 6.2 per cent of total LDC exports, as compared to 24.6 per cent for the 'other developing' group of LDCs. Up to 1972, the share of the major oil exporters had not changed significantly, although the share of the 'other developing' LDCs had more than halved. Between 1972 and 1980, the share of the major oil exporters increased rapidly and accounted for 16.2 per cent of the total by the latter date. The share of the 'other developing' group registered a slight rise during the same period.
b There was no marked trend with respect to the share in total exports of the socialist economies. Their share rose between 1950 and 1960 but declined thereafter, and by 1980 their share was only slightly higher than it had been in 1950. The pattern for their imports was similar.

3 *Table 9.3:* The data clearly illustrate the dominant position of the MDCs in the total export trade of all LDCs, although their share of total non-fuel exports has fallen over the period 1955–78 (from 76.3 per cent to 65.4 per cent). The share of the MDCs of LDC manufactured goods exports has, however, increased quite dramatically, and the MDCs in 1978 accounted for almost (or approximately) two-thirds of LDC manufactured goods exports.

4 *Table 9.4:*
a In 1980, the major oil exporters had a positive trade balance (trade surplus) of $112.4 billion. By 1983, however, the former had fallen to $84.5 billion and the latter to $12.8 billion. Although these figures represent a significant deterioration, it is, nevertheless, important to note that the major oil exporters still maintained a balance of payments surplus in 1983.
b For example, for the net oil-importing group of LDCs, the current account deficit increased from −$64.8 billion in 1980 to −$72.4 billion in 1983.
c In 1980, the exporters of manufactured goods had a current account deficit of $28.3 billion. By 1983, the deficit had fallen to $24.5 billion.

d The seventh column in Table 9.4 (headed total capital flows (net)) clearly illustrates the increasing dependence of most LDCs on capital inflows. The exceptions to this generalisaton are the major oil exporters.

Unit 10 Stage 1

Comprehension questions

A1 F **2** T **3** F **4** T **5** T **6** T

B1 A price rise is simply an increase in the price of a commodity. An inflationary spiral is the process over a period whereby a price rise is accompanied by higher wages which in turn increase the cost of production, thus causing prices to rise again.
2 Because of the inclusion in the groups of Argentina and Brazil, who always seem to have high rates of price increase.
3a Major exporters of manufactures.
b Net oil exporters.
c Western hemisphere.
4 They all experienced inflation, but not at the same rate.
5a Asia.
b Low-income countries.
6 Not explicitly, but by implication i.e. whenever China is included in a set of figures, the percentage is lower; when China is excluded, the figure is higher
e.g. 1981 Low-income countries   9.6 per cent
        excluding China   17.6 per cent

Word study

Exercise 1A Alternative vocabulary

1 d   **3** a   **5** c
2 f   **4** e   **6** b

Exercise 1B Explanation

1 A situation in which prices and wages rise in turn with increases in the supply of money.
2 The price charged by wholesalers for commodities sold in large quantities usually for resale by retailers.

Language use

Exercise 1 Commenting on data (continued)

1a For the non-oil LDCs, excluding China, the average rate of inflation for the period 1968–72 was 9.1 per cent *per annum*. In 1973, the rate of inflation jumped to 22.1 per cent and rose even higher to 28.7 per cent in 1974. Throughout the remainder of the 1970s, the rate of inflation remained in the 20–30 per cent *per annum* range, but in 1980 the rate rose to 36.9 per cent and in 1981 it rose further to 37.2 per cent.
b The major exporters of manufactured goods experienced a rapid acceleration in the rate of inflation in the period covered by the table. From an average annual rate of inflation during 1968–72 of 14.1 per cent, the rate of inflation reached a high of 55.8 per cent in 1976, and although there was a fall in the rate between 1977 and 1979, the early 1980s witnessed a further rise in the rate, to 62.2 per cent in 1981.

c The data clearly show that the western hemisphere had the highest rate of inflation. It averaged 15.3 per cent *per annum* over the period 1968–72 (as compared to an average of less than 10 per cent *per annum* for both oil and non-oil LDCs) and during the 1970s, the rate was two-to-three times as high as that of the region with the next highest rate of inflation (the Middle East). By 1981, the western hemisphere rate of inflation was 65.7 per cent, compared to 32.8 per cent for the Middle East and less than 30 per cent for all other developing regions.

d The African region traditionally enjoyed a low rate of inflation (less than 5 per cent *per annum* over the period 1968–72, for example). The rate began to rise in the mid-1970s, however, reaching 19.3 per cent in 1977. A slight fall in 1978 was followed by further rises in subsequent years and, by 1981, the rate of inflation had reached 22.7 per cent.

2 The rate of inflation for Asia, excluding China, exhibits a pattern common to most LDCs. Relatively low rates in the 1960s were followed by an acceleration in the 1970s, although in the case of Asia, the highest rate of inflation (30.3 per cent) was experienced slightly earlier (1974) than in other regions (1975 or 1976). 1976 saw a dramatic fall in the rate of inflation and it remained at relatively low levels for the remainder of the 1970s. In common with other LDCs, it rose in 1980, but fell slightly in 1981.

If we compare Asia with Europe, we can see an initially lower rate of acceleration until 1974 in the case of the latter region, but subsequently a less dramatic fall in 1975 and 1976. Thereafter, the rate of inflation for Europe rises until 1980 and is always significantly higher than Asia's rate of inflation.

Unit 10   Stage 2

Comprehension

Post-questions

1a Because the supply curve at this point is still horizontal (there is still productive capacity to be utilised).

b Because the supply curve becomes vertical at point Y_3 thus causing any further increase in demand to increase prices.

2 Structural bottlenecks or constraints. The three main ones are: the agricultural sector bottleneck, the foreign exchange bottleneck and the budget deficit bottleneck.

3 Because econometric testing has tended to favour the monetarist explanation of inflation in LDCs. This is particularly because of the close correlation between money supply and prices. In addition structuralist hypotheses are very difficult to test empirically.

4 Because it ignores the internal structures of LDCs and differences in those structures between LDCs. How far an LDC can be affected by imported inflationary pressures depends on a number of factors. A model needs to cater for these (e.g. identifying, measuring and relating the most important constraints to the level and strategy of development chosen).

Word study

Exercise 1A Alternative vocabulary

1 d	4 i	7 a	10 o	13 p	16 c
2 f	5 l	8 m	11 b	14 h	17 g
3 k	6 j	9 e	12 n	15 q	

Exercise 1B Explanation

1 The national budget sets out estimates of government expenditure and revenue for the financial year.

2 Consisting of, or capable of being easily converted into, cash.

3 A series of events taking place in a regularly repeated order.

4 A sudden rapid growth and expansion of economic activity.

5 A period of reduced economic activity (from the verb 'to recede').

6 Mutual relationship; a statistical technique for determining the extent to which variations in the values of one variable are associated with variations in values of another.

7 Departing from the norm; the difference between a single value in a series of numbers and the average (mean) of those numbers.

8 The number or mathematical quantity by which a variable is multiplied.

Language use

Exercise 2 Academic caution

Various answers are possible e.g.
Inflation *appears to* be a problem for LDCs.
Inflation is *almost certainly* a problem for LDCs.
Inflation *may well* be a problem for LDCs.

Index to language use exercises

Units and stages in which they appear

Appendices

Appendix 1 Study skills

A Note-taking **B** Writing an essay **C** Referencing

A Note-taking

In note-taking the main points are written briefly, in words or phrases. Frequently, abbreviations are used: e.g. 'econ.' for 'economic' and 'dev(t).' for 'development'. Symbols often indicate the connections between ideas

e.g.

∴   therefore
∵   because
+   and/plus
÷   division/divided
→   leads to/results in/causes
=   is equal to/equals
≡   the same as/identical to
>   bigger/larger/greater than
<   smaller/less than

(A more detailed account of note-taking, together with practice, is given in James, K., Jordan, R. R., and Matthews, A. J. (1979) *Listening Comprehension and Note-Taking Course*, London, Collins ELT.)
Below are shown two different ways of taking notes: each one is based on the text in Unit 1 Stage 2 *Economic development*.

Econ. Devt.

1 In early years, econ. growth & econ. dev^t. = synonymous.
But – GNP per capita = a poor indicator of econ. welfare & the level of econ. dev^t.
– over time → econ. growth = nec. cond^n. but not a suffict. cond^n. for increases in econ. welfare.

2 Later, econ. dev^t. includes progress.
∴ econ. dev^t. = growth + structural/institut^{nl} change → certain normative objectives
Growth without dev^t. was a possibility if there were no struct^l. changes to go with increases in per capita income etc. – but growth inevitably leads to changes in econ. structure – ∴ 'growth + change' = not helpful.

3 Normative defin. of dev^t. – most widely used = of Dudley Seers – 'dev^t. = normative concept→synonym for improve^{t}.'
Criteria = poverty, inequality, unemploy^t. – other indicators = political, social & educational dimensions of dev^t. – also reducing cultural dependence on a great power – ∴ self-reliance = important element in dev^t.

4 Difficulties = assess extent objectives realised.
Hicks & Streeten → 4 diff. approaches to the problem of measure^t.
a adjustments to GNP   **c** social a/c systems
b social indicators   **d** composite indices
– but they are all unsatis. in some way.

5 Recognit^n. that econ. growth does not auto. solve problems relating to poverty, inequality & unemploy^t. = imp. step forward.
But Seers-type defins. of dev^t. refer to ideal world ∴ = ahistorical & apolitical.
World ÷ = DCs & LDCs – utilis^n. of idealised dev^t. concept implies DCs solved problems of dev^t. – not true. Also, normative dev^t. concept denies specificity of processes of growth and change occurring in LDCs.
An alternative way to make notes: branching notes
(The title is indicated in the loop in the centre. The notes start with (1) – at the top, right, and read clockwise round to (5). After reading each number, the lettered sub-divisions of each, (a), (b), (c) etc., should be read, reading from the centre outwards.)

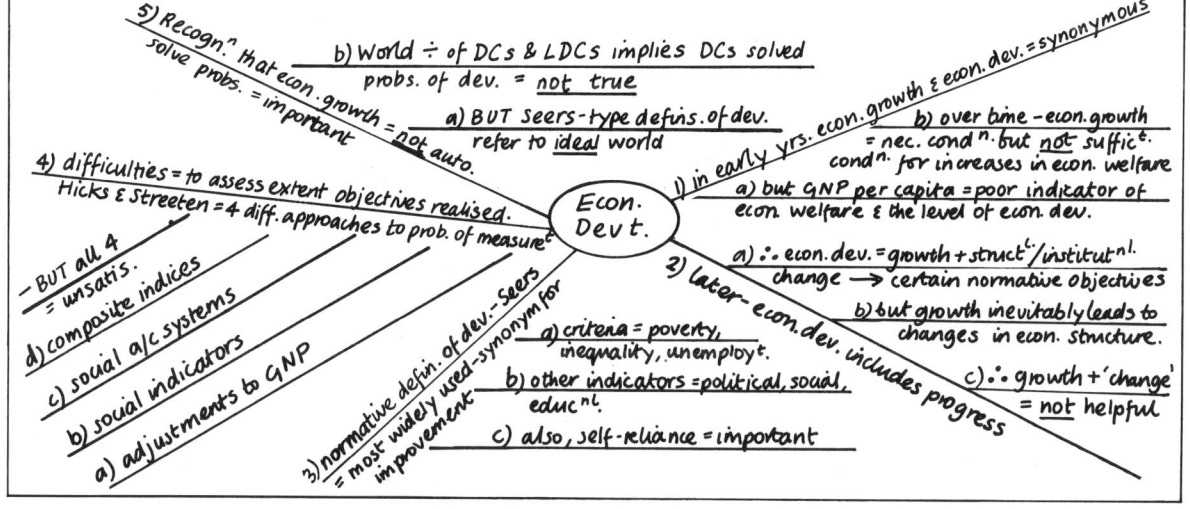

B   Writing an essay

Below is some general advice on writing an academic essay. Always make sure that you understand exactly what the question or title means and requires before you begin to write. A very useful book that gives practice in this is Howe, P. M., (1983) *Answering Examination Questions*, Glasgow, Collins ELT. A book that gives more practice in academic essay writing is Jordan, R. R., (1980) *Academic Writing Course*, London, Collins ELT.

1 Spend three or four minutes thinking about your essay: what to include, how to begin, how to conclude. Make a few rough notes of the content and structure of the essay.

2 The essay should be clearly organised into paragraphs, and the paragraphs organised into three main sections:

> Introduction: one (or more) paragraph(s)
> Development: several paragraphs
> Conclusion: one (or more) paragraph(s)

3 The introduction may be written in a number of ways depending on the topic or question e.g. by giving a definition of the subject, by giving brief background information or by explaining the scope or limitations of the subject or answer.

> It is essential that the introductory paragraph is written clearly and that it creates a favourable impression upon the reader. Ideally, the introductory paragraph should:
> 1 indicate that the question has been understood and that you can interpret it;
> 2 indicate the structure and sequence of the answer;
> 3 indicate the content.
> It should be relatively short: perhaps not more than about fifteen lines or so.

4 Try to remember the 4 Cs when writing your essay:

> Clear   →writing and expression of ideas (easy to read and understand)
> Comprehensive→all the main ideas and arguments are included
> Concise   →short and precise (no unnecessary repetition)
> Correct   →accurate – both in content and in language use

5 Below is an example of the outline and notes for an essay: the title is the one given in Extension activities in Unit 1 Stage 2:

'What are the main problems associated with economic development?'

Introduction
What does the essay title mean (or answer require)?
– is the essay about how to *define* economic development, or how to *achieve* economic development?
– assume essay is concerned with *definition* of economic development
– note various definitions that have been given in the past: the problem is therefore one of selection – which definition is most useful or relevant for our purpose?

Development
– economic growth as a necessary but not sufficient condition to ensure increases in economic and social welfare
– economic development therefore taken to mean growth plus structural change
– but: can the two be separated?
– move to normative definitions of development; problems associated with their use
– attempts made to measure realisation of development objectives

Conclusion
review of questions raised – problems not solved – alternative conceptions/definitions of development – validity/relevance of alternative concepts – can 'development' be measured? Personal views of student on these questions.

C   Referencing

1 Footnotes   2 Quotations   3 References/Bibliographies

1   Footnotes

A small number written above a word or item of information in the text means that there is a special note about it. The note is often at the bottom or foot of the page: thus it is called a *footnote*. If there are two or more footnotes then they are numbered in sequence 1, 2, 3, etc. If they appear at the foot of each page, the numbering starts anew on each page. If they appear at the end of an essay, the numbering is continuous throughout the essay.

2   Quotations

When referring to a book or article in an essay, the normal procedure is to give the author's surname, the year of publication in brackets, and the page numbers if possible. The full reference is then given at the end of the essay.

There are three basic ways of using quotations in an essay:

a *quotation marks around the author's words which are then incorporated in the text*; this is often used for short quotations:
. . . (Seers, 1979, pp. 27–28), a further dimension is added – 'development now implies, inter alia, reducing cultural dependence on one or more of the great powers'. Self reliance thus becomes . . .

b *the quotation is indented* (i.e. it starts further from the margin than the other lines – and it may be in a different type size or style):
For Seers,
'"Development" is inevitably a normative concept, almost a synonym for improvement. To pretend otherwise is just to hide one's value judgements.'
(Seers, 1972, p. 22)
Posing the question . . .

c *a paraphrase* (i.e. rewriting the author's words):
Hicks and Streeten (1979, p. 568) identify and review four different approaches to the problem of measurement, namely: . . .

3   References/Bibliographies

References, at the end of an essay, for example, are arranged in alphabetical order (A–Z) of the author's surname or the name of the organization. If more than one reference is given by the same author, then the earlier dated reference will appear first.

a Note the following sequence of information commonly used in references to *books*: Author's surname, initials, (date – in brackets), *title* (underlined or in italics), place of publication, publisher.

e.g.

Frank, A. G. (1967), *Capitalism and Underdevelopment in Latin America*, New York, Monthly Review Press.

b In references to *articles in journals* there are some differences in the information given:

Author's surname, initials, (date – in brackets), title of article, *name of journal* (underlined or in italics), volume number, issue number, sometimes season or month, sometimes page numbers.

e.g.

Hicks, N. & Streeten, P. (1979), 'Indicators of Development: The Search for a Basic Needs Yardstick', *World Development*, Vol. 7, No. 6, June.

Further information about, and practice in, referencing is given in O'Brien, Teresa, and Jordan, R. R. (1985), *Developing Reference Skills*, London, Collins ELT.

Appendix 2   Abbreviations of economics terms and organisations

(Those used in this book are indicated by the Unit and Stage number where they first occur.)

ADB	– African Development Bank; Asian Development Bank
APC	– average propensity to consume
APS	– average propensity to save
ASEAN	– Association of South East Asian Nations
BIS	– Bank of International Settlements
CACM	– Central American Common Market
CDC	– Commonwealth Development Corporation
cif	– cost, insurance, freight
DC	– Developed Country
DFI	– direct foreign investment (7.2)
ECSC	– European Coal and Steel Community
EEC	– European Economic Community ('the Common Market')
EFTA	– European Free Trade Associaton
EPU	– European Payments Union
FAO	– Food and Agricultural Organisation (of the UN)
fob	– free on board
GATT	– General Agreement on Tariffs and Trade
GDP	– Gross Domestic Product (1.1)
GCFC	– gross fixed capital formation
GNP	– Gross National Product (1.1)
IBRD	– International Bank for Reconstruction and Development (the World Bank)
ICOR	– incremental capital output ratio
IDA	– International Development Association
ILO	– International Labour Organisation/Office (4.2)
IMF	– International Monetary Fund (9.2)
ISI	– import-substituting industrialisation (6.2)
ISIC	– International Standard Industrial Classification
LAFTA	– Latin American Free Trade Association
LDC	– Less Developed Country (1.1)
MNC	– multinational corporation
MPC	– marginal propensity to consume
MPS	– marginal propensity to save
NI	– National Income (1.1)
NIC	– Newly Industrialising Country (6.2)
NNP	– Net National Product (1.1)
OECD	– Organisation for Economic Cooperation and Development (8.2)
OPEC	– Organisation of Petroleum Exporting Countries (7.2)
R & D	– research and development (7.2)
SCB	– social cost–benefit (analysis) (3.2)
SDR	– special drawing rights
SIC	– Standard Industrial Classification
TNC	– transnational corporation (6.2)
UN	– United Nations (7.1)
UNCTAD	– United Nations Conference on Trade and Development (9.2)
UNESCO	– United Nations Educational, Scientific and Cultural Organisation
UNIDO	– United Nations Industrial Development Organisation (6.1)
US	– United States (of America) (7.1)
VAT	– value added tax
WHO	– World Health Organisation

Appendix 3 Mathematical expressions in economics

The purpose of this Appendix is not to show the use of equations, but to show how to verbalise (say) them in English. We start with the letters of the Greek alphabet that are commonly used in equations.

Students can practise in pairs or in a group by trying to read out Part 1, and being corrected by someone checking with Part 2. Alternatively, one person can read out Part 2 and the other student(s) can try to write the appropriate symbol.

Note the names of the brackets.

$$(\quad)\qquad[\quad]\qquad\{\quad\}$$
brackets or   square   curly
round brackets brackets brackets

Part 1

1 α β γ Δ/δ ϵ η θ λ μ π ρ Σ/σ ϕ χ Ω

2 x^2 x^3 x^4 x^6

3 $\sqrt{x}$ $\sqrt[3]{x}$ $\sqrt[5]{x}$ $\sqrt[10]{x}$

4 x' x''' x^{-1} $(x'x)^{-1}$ $\bar{x}$ $\hat{x}$ χ^2 $\tilde{x}$ x^* $\bar{\bar{x}}$

5 x_{ij}^n a_0

6 $\dfrac{dx}{dt}$ $\dfrac{\delta x}{\delta t}$

7 $\sum\limits_{t=1}^{n} yt$ $\int\limits_{-\infty}^{+\infty}$ $\int\limits_{a}^{b}$

8 $\int\limits_{c}^{d}\int\limits_{a}^{b} f(x,y)\,dx\,dy$

9 I_n

10 $(x'x)^{-1}\,x'y$

11 $E(u) = 0$ $E(uu') = \sigma^2 I$

12 $V(x)$

13 $x \sim N[\mu, \sigma^2]$ $u \sim N[0,1]$

14 $(ax)^2$ $[ac - bd]/e^2$ $(a+b)\{(x-y)^2 + 3\}$ $(c+d)$

15 $5!$ $12!$

16 $\prod\limits_{i=1}^{n} a_i$

17 $\sum\limits_{t=0}^{n-1} \dfrac{Rt}{(1+i)^{t+1}} = \sum\limits_{t=0}^{n-1} \dfrac{Et}{(1+i)^{t+1}}$

18 $\sum\limits_{i=1}^{m}\ \sum\limits_{j=1}^{n} x_{ij}$

19 $G = 5{\cdot}2\ (y \times 10^{-6})^{1{\cdot}202} \left(\dfrac{y}{p}\right)^{-0{\cdot}164}$

    $S = 163{\cdot}7\ (y \times 10^{-6})^{1{\cdot}314} \left(\dfrac{y}{p}\right)^{-0{\cdot}655}$

20 $M_1 - M_0 = m_1 S_1 - m_0 S_0$
             $= S_1(m_1 - m_0) + m_0(S_1 - S_0)$

  $[S_1(m_1 - m_0)]$

  $\dfrac{S_1(m_1 - m_0)}{Qt - Q_0}$

  $Q_1 - Q_0 = S_1(1 - m_1) - S_0(1 - m_0)$

  $\dfrac{m_1 - m_0}{m_0}$

21 r_{xy}

22 $\text{cov}(x,y)$

Part 2

1 alpha, beta, gamma, delta (both capital and small letters), epsilon, eta, theta, lambda, mu, pi, rho, sigma (both capital and small letters), phi, chi, omega

2 x squared; x cubed; x to the fourth; x to the sixth

3 square root of x; the cubed root of x; the fifth root of x; the tenth root of x

4 x dash, or x transpose, or x prime; x triple dash; x inverse; x dash x, inverse; x tilde; x hat; chi squared; x bar; x star; x double bar

5 x subscript ij superscript n, or xij to the nth; a zero, or a nought

6 dx by dt; del x by del t

7 sigma from t equals one up to n of yt; the integral from minus infinity to plus infinity; the integral from a to b

8 double integrate the function f over x and y, where x is integrated between a, b, and y between c, d

9 Identity matrix of order n

10 x dash x inverse, x dash y

11 the expectation of u equals zero, or eu equals zero; the expectation of u and u prime equals sigma squared I

12 variance of x

13 x is normally distributed with mean mu and variance sigma squared; u is normally distributed with mean zero and variance one

14 ax all squared; ac minus bd all over e squared; a plus b, curly brackets, x minus y all squared, plus three, end curly brackets, c plus d

15 five factorial; twelve factorial

16 pi from i equals one up to n, ai

17 sigma from t equals zero up to n minus one, Rt over one plus i to the power t plus one equals sigma from t equals zero up to n minus one, Et over one plus i to the power t plus one

18 double sum $x\,ij$ over i and j, where i runs from one to m and j runs from one to n

19 G equals five point two, times y, times ten to the minus six, all to the power one point two oh two, times y over p all to the power minus zero point one six four
S equals one hundred and sixty three point seven times y times ten to the power minus six, all to the one point three one four, times y over p all to the power minus zero point six five five

20 M one minus M zero equals small m one S one minus small m zero S zero equals S one times, small m one minus small m zero, plus, small m zero times S one minus S zero
S one times, m one minus m zero
S one times, m one minus m zero all over Qt minus Q zero
Q one minus Q zero equals S one times, one minus m one, minus S zero times, one minus m zero
m one minus m zero all over m zero

21 correlation coefficient between x and y

22 covariance between x and y

Glossary of Latin phrases and abbreviations commonly used in economics

a fortiori – with stronger reason
a posteriori – from the latter, from effect to cause
a priori – from the former, from cause to effect
ceteris paribus – other things being equal (3.1)
cf.→confer – compare with
e.g.→exempli gratia – for example, for instance
et al. – and others; especially when listing authors, (4.1)
et seq.→et sequens – and the following (pages)
etc.→etcetera – and the rest or others, and so on (2.1)
ex ante – intended, desired or expected before the event. Thus, *ex ante* demand is the quantity which buyers wish or intend to buy at a certain price. (10.2)
ex post – This is the outcome which actually occurs e.g. the actual quantity bought. (10.2)
ibid.→ibidem – in the same place
i.e.→id est – which is to say, in other words, that is
inter- – between, among, e.g. international (between countries) (8.2 and 10.2)
inter alia – among(st) other things (1.2)
intra- – within, inside e.g. intranational (within one country) (10.2)

ipso facto – obvious from the facts
loc. cit.→loco citato – in the places mentioned
modus operandi – a method of working, a system
mutatis mutandis – with due alteration of details (3.1)
N.B.→nota bene – take special note of, note well
non sequitur – it does not follow logically
op. cit.→opere citato – in the work already named
p.a.→per annum – by the year (6.1)
pari passu – with equal speed or progress, side-by-side
per capita – of or for each person; *per capita income*: the total income of a group divided by the number of people in the group. (1.1)
per se – by or in itself; intrinsically (6.2)
post- – after (following) e.g. post-war
pre- – before (in advance) e.g. pre-war
prima facie – at first sight, on first consideration
pro forma – as a matter of form
q.v.→quod vide – which may be referred to, refer to, see (often used for cross-references)
status quo – the existing state of affairs
via – by way of, by means of, through

Glossary of economics terms

1 A note on dictionaries for economists

1 *The Penguin Dictionary of Economics*, 3rd edn., 1984 (edited by G. Bannock, R. E. Baxter and R. Rees), Harmondsworth, Penguin Books.
2 *Macmillan Dictionary of Modern Economics*, revised 1983 (edited by D. W. Pearce), London & Basingstoke, Macmillan.

Of more general interest are:

3 *Longman Dictionary of Business English*, 1982 (edited by J. H. Adam), Harlow, Longman York Press.
4 *Reuters Glossary of International Economic and Financial Terms*, 1982, London, Heinemann.
5 *Collins Business English Dictionary*, 1984 (compiled by M. J. Wallace and P. J. Flynn), London and Glasgow, Collins ELT.

On a larger scale, there is:

6 *Encyclopedia of Economics*, 1982 (edited by D. Greenwald), New York, McGraw-Hill.

2 A note on the economics terms

The following economics terms are to be found in this book. If a term is not included here the student is recommended to refer to one of the dictionaries listed above. If a term is already clearly explained in the book, a simple reference is given to the Unit and Stage in which the term is used. Otherwise the terms are explained here.

aggregate demand (10.2) – The total demand for goods and services in the economy.
aggregate supply (10.2) – The total supply of goods and services in the economy.
aggregation (3.1 – Word study).
assets (4.1 – Word study).
balance of payments (6.2 – Word study & 9.2) – A tabulation of the credit and debit transactions of a country with other countries and international

institutions:
current account: consists of *visible* trade (exports and imports) and *invisible* trade (services, tourism, etc.)
capital account: consists of the inward and outward flow of money for investments and international grants and loans.
boom (10.2 – Word study).
Bretton Woods System (10.2) – (see also *World Bank*) – Under the rules of the IMF, international exchange rates were fixed in relation to the US dollar, and the dollar was convertible into gold at a fixed rate. In 1972–3 the system was suspended : gold convertibility and fixed exchange rates ceased – they were replaced by floating exchange rates.
budget (10.2 – Word study).

co-efficient (10.2 – Word study).
commodity terms of trade (net barter) (9.1)
comparative advantage (9.1)   The specialisation in the production and export of those commodities in which a country is relatively efficient.
constant prices (6.1 – Word study)
correlation (10.2 – Word study)
cost of living index (or retail price index) (10.1) – A measure of the relative changes in prices of a specified set of consumer goods which would be bought by an average household on a regular basis.
cost-push (inflation) (10.2) – Inflation which is created and sustained by increases in production costs, independently of the state of demand.
cycle (10.2 – Word study).

deficit financing (10.2) – A situation where expenditure exceeds revenue such that a deficit is operated deliberately. It is intended to stimulate economic activity and employment by injecting more purchasing power into the economy.
demand-pull (inflation) (10.2) – Inflation created and sustained by an excess of aggregate demand over total

supply of goods and services which can be produced by a fully employed economy (aggregate supply).

dependency (2.2) – The structure of economic, social, political and military relationships with which the interests of the LDCs are subservient to the interests of the developed capitalist economies.

depreciation (1.1) – A reduction in the value of assets from wear and tear.

direct foreign investment (DFI) (7.2) – The investment in productive assets by a company in a country (host country) other than its country of origin or domicile (home country).

discounting (3.2) – The process of applying a rate of interest (discount rate) to a capital sum. It is generally used to find the present value of sums receivable or payable in the future.

disguised unemployment (5.2 – Word study).

division of labour (2.1 – Word study).

durable consumer goods (9.1 – Word study).

econometrics (8.2) – The application of mathematical and statistical techniques to economic problems.

economic development (1.2)

economic growth (1.1)

economic surplus (2.2) – (as defined by neo-Marxists) The difference between what is produced (output) and current consumption; potential economic surplus = the difference between output that *could* be produced in a given natural and technological environment and what is regarded as essential consumption.

economic welfare (1.2) – That part of human welfare which results from the consumption of goods and services.

entrepreneur (2.2 – Word study).

factors of production (8.2 – Word study).

factor substitutability (8.2) – The use of different combinations of factors of production (usually capital and labour) as their relative prices vary.

functional distribution of income (4.2) – Income is divided according to its source (arising from ownership of land, capital and labour).

Gross Domestic Product (GDP) (1.1)

Gross National Product (GNP) (1.1)

household (4.1 – Word study).

import-substituting industrialisation (ISI) (6.2)

income elasticity of demand (8.2) – Responsiveness of the demand for a good to changes in the buyer's income.

index/indices (1.2) – An index number is a single number which gives the average value of a set of related items expressed as a percentage of their average value at some base period.

indirect taxes (1.1 – Word study)

inflation (10.1)

inflationary spiral (10.1 – Word study) – An inflationary situation which encourages employees to demand higher wages which in turn increases cost of production, and hence prices increase even further.

infrastructure (2.2 – Word study)

internalisation of assets (7.2) – When the market is costly and inefficient for certain kinds of transactions, the firm will organise and carry out those transactions at a lower cost within the firm rather than through the market i.e. the transactions are internalised and undertaken by the firm itself.

Keynesian economics (3.2) – Keynes, John Maynard (1883–1946) : English economist. In his book *The General Theory of Employment, Interest and Money* (1936) he advocated the use of government fiscal and monetary policy to adjust demand and maintain full employment without inflation (known as 'Keynesianism'). Keynes, in effect, laid the foundations for macro-economics.

labour-intensive (3.2)

lagged effects (10.2) – A relationship between a set of variables in which the current value of the dependent variable is related to previous values of one or more independent variables.

liquidity (10.2 – Word study).

macro-economics (3.1) – The study of the behaviour of the economy as a whole; that part of economics which is concerned with the study of relationships between broad economic aggregates – national income, savings, investment, employment, money supply etc.

marginal productivity (5.2) – Of labour or capital – an increase in output resulting from increasing labour (or capital) input by a small amount.

Marx, Karl (2.2) – (1818–83). German founder of modern communism; lived in England from 1849. With Engels he wrote *The Communist Manifesto* (1848). He developed his theories of the class struggle and the economics of capitalism in *Das Kapital* (1867; 1885; 1895).

micro-economics (3.1) – That part of economics which is concerned with the study of individual decision units – consumers and firms.

monetarism (3.2) – A particular approach to macro-economic theory which argues that disturbances within the monetary sector are the main cause of instability in the economy.

monetarist (3.2) – One who believes in monetarism.

monopolistic (6.2 – Word study).

National Income (N.I.) (1.1) – A measure of the money value of the total flow of goods and services produced in an economy over a specified period.

neo-classical (3.2) – A body of economic theory using the general approach and techniques of 19th century marginalist economists, largely concerned with the efficient allocation of scarce resources.

neo-Marxism (2.2)

net (1.1) – What remains after all deductions have been made (e.g. taxes, expenses) e.g. net profit (= after tax, rent, etc. are paid). *Gross* profit = total profit.

net barter (9.1) – see *commodity terms of trade*.

Net National Product (NNP) (1.1) – GNP less depreciation.

non-equity operations (7.2) – Overseas operations by TNCs that do not involve a long-term ownership interest by one enterprise in another; examples of non-equity operations are licensing, management contracts, franchising, international subcontracting.

normative (1.2) – concerned with values, opinions of what *ought* to be rather than what is (see *welfare economics*). Thus, normative propositions would be: unemployment is too high; inflation ought to be stopped.

oligopoly (7.2 – Word study).

open economy (3.1 – Word study).

parameter (3.1) – A specified term in an equation; a quantity which remains constant in a given context.

Phillips curve (10.2)

price expectations (10.2) – Beliefs or views on the future growth of prices.

price mechanism (3.2) – The system of resource allocation which is based on the free movement of prices.

primary products (3.1 – Word study).

production function (8.2) – A mathematical relationship between the quantity of output of a good and the quantity of inputs required to make it.

proxy variable (10.2) – A variable used in regression analysis to replace or 'stand in for' another more theoretically satisfactory variable which is either not measurable or for which data are not available.

real income (1.1 – footnote).

recession (10.2 – Word study).

shadow price (3.2) – The imputed valuation of a commodity or service; the true marginal value which may differ from market price, used in SCB.

size distribution of income (4.2) – It refers to the distribution of income regardless of source; it shows how many persons (or families) receive how much income.

social accounts (1.2) – The presentation of national income and expenditure accounts in a form showing the transactions during a given period between different sectors of the economy.

social cost–benefit analysis (SCB) (3.2) – A technique which attempts to set out and evaluate the social costs and social benefits of investment projects.

social opportunity cost (3.2) – The losses and gains in economic welfare which are incurred by society as a whole if a particular project is undertaken.

structural bottleneck (10.2)

structuralist (3.2)

tariff barriers (6.2 – Word study).

tax havens (7.2 – Word study).

technical rigidity (8.2)

terms of trade (6.2 – Word study).

transfer prices (7.2) – Intra-firm prices i.e. the prices that are charged for transactions that take place within the firm. *Transfer pricing* is the system of setting prices for transactions among subsidiaries or between the parent company and subsidiaries of a TNC where the prices are not subject to market determination.

transnational corporation (7.1)

urban informal sector (5.2)

U-shaped relationship (4.2) – A presumed inverse relationship between *per capita* income and some measure of inequality in size distribution of income.

value added (6.1) – (or net output) – The difference between total revenue and the cost of bought-in raw materials, services and components; it measures the value that a firm has 'added' to these items in the process of production.

variable (3.1) – A number capable of taking different values.

weak currencies (7.2 – Word study).

welfare economics (3.2) – That branch of economics which is concerned with normative issues; it is concerned with economic efficiency, resource allocation, social welfare.

wholesale price (10.1 – Word study).

World Bank (1.1) – another name for the International Bank for Reconstruction and Development (IBRD), whose establishment was agreed upon, along with the International Monetary Fund (IMF), at the UN Monetary and Financial Conference at Bretton Woods, USA, in 1944. It began operations in 1946. Its main purpose is to encourage capital investment in LDCs, either through channelling private funds, or through making loans from its own resources.

Word study: index to explanation exercises

Unit and stage numbers given

1.1 any given year
indirect taxes

1.2 value judgements
criteria
common denominator

2.1 vicious circle
opposite sides of the same coin
spheres of interest
captive markets
division of labour

2.2 infrastructure
entrepreneur
blocked
accumulated
static

3.1 open economy
primary products
aggregation

3.2 empirical evidence
shadow prices
labour-intensive techniques of production

4.1 household
the poor are disproportionately located in rural areas
assets
the 'required' intake

4.2 in the latter than in the former
a trade-off
a partial determinant

5.1 one billion

5.2 disguised unemployment
recycling

6.1 constant prices

6.2 tariff barriers
monopolistic
terms of trade
balance of payments

7.1 host countries

7.2 extractive sectors
product differentiation
oligopoly
weak currencies
brand names and trade marks

8.1 capital goods
intermediate goods

8.2 factors of production
ratio
point of tangency
consumption

9.1 durable consumer goods
hypothesis

9.2 the post-war period
fuel
to service the debts

10.1 an inflationary spiral
wholesale price

10.2 budget
liquidity
cycle
boom
recession
correlation
deviation
coefficient

Word study: index to alternative vocabulary exercises

List of words and units and stages in which they appear